Graduate Study
in the Liberal Arts College

FREDERIC W. NESS

and

BENJAMIN D. JAMES

*for the Commission on Professional
and Graduate Study*

ASSOCIATION OF AMERICAN COLLEGES
1962

Graduate Study
in the Liberal Arts College

Foreword

The rising demand for graduate education, which is simply a reflection of the national need for more and more highly trained personnel, is felt not only in the larger private and public universities. As has been evident for some time, a substantial number of our independently structured colleges as well have had an active interest in this development. Since many of these are among the liberal arts colleges which comprise a high percentage of the constituency of the Association of American Colleges, and since inevitably those conducting graduate programs share many problems in common, the Association, through its Commission on Professional and Graduate Study, concurred in the desirability of providing some means of pooling the experiences of these colleges both for their mutual benefit and for the guidance of others which may be contemplating the inauguration of graduate programs.

The result is the following descriptive and evaluative study, made possible through the generosity of the Lilly Endowment, Inc. Our appreciation goes both to the endowment and to the authors, Vice President Ness and Dean James, who labored fruitfully in a relatively uncultivated vineyard.

THEODORE A. DISTLER
Association of American Colleges

v

Contents

List of Tables

List of Figures

CHAPTER I

Graduate Study
and the Liberal Arts College

When many of the older colleges included in this study were established, their founders were not consciously giving life to what today would be recognized under the rubric of the small, independent, liberal arts college. As their charters in many instances show, the aspirations of these fledglings were almost unlimited. They intended to provide programs and offer degrees similar to those available in any of the leading institutions of Europe and America. Whether the subsequent limiting factors were matters of geography, economics, ineluctable chance, or, to grant the most favorable interpretation, deliberate design, these institutions remained relatively small and homogeneous, while at the same time many of their contemporaries burgeoned into the multifaceted colossi which they are today.

Even in America the distinction between a *college* and a *university* is not necessarily to be found in the title, for there are colleges which exceed in size many of our smaller universities. Moreover, the college is not necessarily limited in its scope, for there are many so-called colleges which have developed a variety of graduate and professional divisions. Generally, however, the distinction between a college and a university is that the former has remained relatively small, retaining more or less its singleness of purpose, while the latter has become many-dimensional, with various graduate or professional divisions emanating from its undergraduate structure.

Thus, when the subject of graduate study in America arises for consideration, one naturally thinks of the universities rather than the colleges, on the assumption that if the colleges are providing any post-baccalaureate work it must be on a very small scale. Although, in general, this assumption is correct, nevertheless the amount of graduate study offered by American colleges—colleges which are essentially small (under 2500), independent, liberal arts, and basically undergraduate in purpose and function—is surprisingly extensive. The survey conducted in preparation for this study revealed that as many as 148 colleges, out of some 623 in this category, are now providing graduate curricula leading to the master's degree.[1]

Nor is the situation static. On the contrary, there is every evidence of a rapidly advancing trend. Eighty-one of these colleges offering graduate programs inaugurated their programs after 1946. The survey further disclosed that another 70 of the colleges in this category are actively considering the establishment in the near future of at least limited graduate offerings, presumably leading to the master's degree, in one or more fields. Thus any consideration of graduate study in America must be cognizant of the substantial opportunities available in institutions which are essentially four-year undergraduate colleges but which, for a variety of reasons, have undertaken or are planning to undertake programs leading to the master's degree.

Through its long history American education has evolved a variety of patterns to meet the demands made upon it by the society it serves. Today it is being challenged to produce more and more graduates with advanced training to satisfy the enlarging requirements of business, government, and education. The challenge is not just to produce more but to produce better-trained men and women for service in these areas. It follows, then, that the facilities of these colleges, to the extent that they are devoted to graduate interests, must be used effectively.

There is some evidence, however, that the graduate work offered by many of the smaller institutions, perhaps even more than in the larger universities, presents difficulty in definition. In some colleges

---

1. See Appendix I for a list of the colleges included in this study. Since only 143 of these provided information, this study is perforce based on those responding rather than on the total number offering graduate study.

2

it is basically an extension of the undergraduate liberal arts program; in others it provides a useful transition between undergraduate and doctoral work; in still others—and these comprise a majority of the institutions included in this study—it represents a specialized, professional preparation for elementary and secondary school teachers. Thus there is a constant danger, in talking about the master's degree in the liberal arts college, of discussing three separate degrees or programs as if they were one. Much of the criticism of the degree, as reviewed in the following pages, in fact stems from these varied functions, whose very diversity has tended to blur the sharp image which the degree created before the introduction, in the last century, of the German Ph.D.

The purpose of this study, which has been sponsored by the Commission on Professional and Graduate Study of the Association of American Colleges, is both to discover the nature and scope of the graduate programs in the private, independently structured colleges and to search for criteria for the maintenance and improvement of their quality. At the very least an effort has been made to bring together in a relatively brief compass some of the more relevant experiences gained by the many colleges which have survived their period of trial and error with graduate study.

Methodology. This study was actively begun in the spring of 1960. An explanatory letter with a return card was sent to the presidents of 623 colleges which seemed to fall within the scope of the survey. The 622 returns revealed that 148 were offering programs leading to the master's degree. As was indicated above, another 70 stated that they were in various stages of planning for master's programs.

During the period of this preliminary identification, a four-page questionnaire was drawn up—perhaps "evolved" would be the more precise word—and submitted to a variety of persons for criticism and review. Even after its initial "dry run," the questionnaire, as is probably more often the case than not, still had a few "bugs" in it when it was finally launched in August of 1960. A copy of the questionnaire has been included in Appendix II.

Despite the surfeit experienced by most academic officials with the spate of questionnaires inundating their offices, 143 of the 148 institutions replied, with only a few of them requiring any special urging.

Where available, the college bulletin or other printed material descriptive of the graduate program was included with the returns.

Since, perforce, the questionnaire could not contain all questions relevant to a thorough survey, a preliminary analysis of the replies was made in order to facilitate the selection of a representative group of colleges for on-the-scene visitation. Then, with the aid of grants from the Association of American Colleges and the Lilly Endowment, visits were made to 42 of the colleges. Although these were selected primarily on a geographical basis, an effort was made to include representatives of different types of institutions and programs within the limits of the over-all study.[2] These investigations were completed between October, 1960, and March, 1961.

The visits, which provided insofar as possible a meeting with each person having substantial responsibility for the graduate program, were characterized by both genuine hospitality and genuine concern, concern for both the local and the national problems of graduate study. Not infrequently divisional or departmental groups were convened to meet with the project representative sometime during his stay on the campus.

After reviewing the questionnaires and the notes on the campus visits, the directors were conscious of two serious lacunae in their data. Their methodology had not provided for adequate expression of opinion from either faculty or students in these graduate programs. To compensate in part for this omission, 50 colleges were selected at random from the total group (by choosing every third college from an alphabetical listing) of institutions in the study; and, again, with the assistance of the directors of the graduate programs, supplementary questionnaires were distributed to two faculty members and two students in each program.[3] Although the local officials were asked to assign the questionnaires on a purely random basis, the procedure here was beyond the control of the directors of the study and thus may not be wholly representative. Nevertheless, a seventy per cent return from these supplementary questionnaires gives reasonable assurance of an undirected and, it is hoped, uninhibited response.

The assembled data were then organized and evaluated, and this report was prepared.

2. See Appendix I.
3. Copies of these questionnaires are included in Appendix II.

The Status of the Master's Degree. To many educational commentators over the past twenty years any study of the master's degree in America would represent an exercise in futility. Although originally on a par with the doctorate—and perhaps much more clearly understood by the public at large—the degree, largely through the lack of effort of the major universities, has lost much of its selective significance. Whereas the Ph.D. has become the acceptable entree to a great variety of professional opportunities, the master's degree, in many institutions, is regarded as the road to preferment for the elementary or secondary school teacher.

Dean Napier Wilt, of the Division of the Humanities of the University of Chicago, talking to the Master of Arts candidates at their convocation in December, 1956, presented them with this encouraging note:

> It is a fact that at many schools students win Bachelor's degrees by doing little more than attend classes over a four-year period. And, although the news will stun those of you who are being awarded A.M.'s today, the truth is that at many schools students win Master's degrees with as little effort. I do not hesitate to say that I can conceive of no student with a Bachelor's degree, however dull, uneducated, stupid, and lazy he may be, who will not be admitted by some graduate school. Moreover, this student will in time be given an A.M. degree or even a doctorate and sent out to teach a subject which he has not even begun to understand.[4]

One can only assume that this was not the situation at Chicago. But he cannot assume that there was anything new in what Dr. Wilt was describing, for a review of the proceedings of the Association of Graduate Schools (in the Association of American Universities) reveals marked concern with the master's degree. For example, in discussing the "Report of the Committee on Policies in Graduate Education," Dean Moody E. Prior, of the Graduate School of Northwestern University, said: "I am very skeptical of being able to rehabilitate this degree in America. There are so many institutions of all sorts giving it, it is given for so many purposes, and there are so many forms of

---

4. Convocation address, "Higher Degrees and Lower Standards," delivered in December, 1956, at the University of Chicago. *Journal of General Education* X (April 1957), p. 99.

accreditation bound to it that I despair of restoring it to anything like intellectual respectability except on a negligible scale." [5]

Not all of the graduate deans at this meeting were quite so discouraging, however. Dean M. E. Hobbs, chairman of the Committee on Policies of the association and dean of the Graduate School of Duke University, said:

> The Ph.D. is a "new" degree, and has never been clearly defined because, as it grew apace, time was not taken to ask what it was and what it should do. The A.M., on the other hand, is a venerable degree and for centuries it was quite clearly understood, until gradually the German-born degree began its encroachments.
>
> At present, requirements for the A.M. vary sharply over the country and as the requirements vary, so does the respect paid the degree. If the A.M. were of universal dignity and good standing and not viewed here and there as a mere "consolation degree" for an unobtainable Ph.D., as just a "quick degree" or as representing a superficial performance, this ancient degree could bring us succor in the decade ahead. If the A.M. were considered as worthy in its way as the Ph.D. in its—each reflecting different amounts of the same thing and not performances different in quality—we might fill our demand for college teachers with men holding the A.M. A grim alternative awaits us—the cheapened, debased Ph.D. or else some new degree, untested and competitive.
>
> The nub of the problem, then, is to get rid of "good" and "bad" A.M.'s and to set up generally a "rehabilitated" degree which will have such worth in its own right that a man entering graduate school will consider the possibility of working toward the A.M. as the first step to the Ph.D. At this point we should add that, if an institution concludes that it cannot, with its limited resources, embark upon the rehabilitated A.M. program, then at least it should refrain from harming the degree by issuing cheap ones.[6]

This was 1957. Certainly no thoughtful observer of the academic scene could see much change in the few intervening years. The call for restraint would seem to be unheeded as more candidates clamor for the master's degree and more colleges and universities devise programs to meet the demand. The graduate chairman in one of the

5. "Report of Committee on Policies in Graduate Education," *Journal of Proceedings and Addresses,* Association of Graduate Schools in the Association of American Universities, 1957, pp. 46-47.
6. *Ibid.,* pp. 40-41.

small colleges included in this survey wrote of his own rather limited program: "Another disadvantage is the growing number of enrollees. The greater number does not permit the degree of individual attention we formerly gave. A much lesser number does not permit as varied course offerings, however." Thus even the smaller graduate programs find themselves caught in a dilemma partially of their own making, a dilemma cogently summed up in the complaint from another dean: "too many people are interested in advanced degrees for prestige and financial reasons only, which makes it difficult to maintain high academic standards."

But the real dilemma may lie much deeper. The fact is that, no matter how diffused the master's degree may have become, we cannot do without it. Not a single proposal for doing away with it, for finding a better substitute for it, or for improving it—and there have been many of each—has met any general acceptance. Many of the long-established universities actively discourage their graduate students from pausing long enough on the road to the doctorate to earn the master's. But there are simply not enough doctorates to go around;[7] this means that education, industry, and government—the chief consumers of highly trained personnel—will continue to compete vigorously for recipients of a degree which the academic world, at least, seems to hold in some disregard.

Nevertheless, the degree continues to thrive, as a way station, and evidently a coveted one, between the baccalaureate and the doctorate.

7.   Dr. Ray Maul analyzes the situation as follows: "Starting with 31.4 percent of the new full-time teachers employed in 1953-54 holding the doctor's degree, the decline in the percent of new teachers entering service with this comprehensive background of preparation dropped alarmingly to 23.5 percent in 1956-57. A year later it climbed a little—to 25.3 percent—but the employment of only 23.8 percent at this level during 1958-59 raises doubt as to whether we have done more than stem the precipitate downtrend.

"Of equal concern is the lack of evidence that the employment of new full-time teachers at the bottom of the preparation scale—below the master's degree level—has been checked. Starting with 18.2 percent in 1954-55, this group increased to 23.1 percent in 1956-57. The 1958-59 figure—20.8 percent—means that 1 of every 5 of the most recently employed full-time teachers in universities and colleges has not yet earned the master's degree."
—*Teacher Supply and Demand in Universities, Colleges, and Junior Colleges, 1957-58 and 1958-59* (Washington: National Education Association, Research Division, 1959), p. 12.

Bernard Berelson, in his provocative analysis in *Graduate Education in the United States*, writes:

> The degree is by no means on its way out. If it were going to die in our generation or the next it would have died already! But it is flourishing: an average in the 1950's of well over 60,000 a year. The reason is simply that it is needed . . . for certifying, for occasional testing, for consoling . . ., for insuring the student against eventualities. And it is worth something on the consuming end, too. After all, a Master's does mean more than "some graduate work." If anything, it is becoming more important in the secondary schools, especially in the growing attractiveness of the Master's with subject matter emphasis as in the Master of Arts in Teaching programs now developing.[8]

There has even been some salutary experimentation directed toward increasing the usefulness of the master's degree. The Master of Arts in Teaching, with substantive levitation from the Ford Foundation, has given something of a new look to one of the degree's many façades; and the same is true of the experimental fifth-year programs which, again with pump-priming from the Ford Foundation, are designed to combine undergraduate and graduate study leading to both the baccalaureate and the first professional degrees. But one cannot help feeling, after reviewing the annual proceedings of such organizations as the Association of Graduate Schools, the Association of American Colleges, the Association for Higher Education, and the like, that very little improvement in the master's degree is likely to come from the larger institutions, especially those awarding the doctorate.

A Degree of Perspective. Samuel Eliot Morison, in *The Development of Harvard University, 1869-1929*, reports that during the first quarter of the nineteenth century the townspeople of Cambridge frequently remarked that "all a Harvard man has to do for his Master's degree is to pay $5.00 and stay out of jail." [9] Nor was this in any sense an exaggeration. Or, if so, it is certainly backed by considerable authority.

8. New York: McGraw-Hill Book Company, 1960; pp. 293-94.
9. Cambridge: Harvard University Press, 1935; p. 452. A brief review of the development of the master's degree is to be found in *Higher Education in Transition,* by John S. Brubacher and Willis Rudy (New York: Harper & Brothers, 1958), pp. 188-89.

Richard J. Storr, in his definitive study *The Beginnings of Graduate Education in America,* writes as follows:

> Many Americans did, of course, take the Master's of Arts degree, qualifying for it by staying alive and out of trouble for three years after graduating from college and by giving very modest evidence of intellectual attainments. Residence as a student in a university was not ordinarily required. . . . Occasionally Bachelors of Arts did linger on about the campus; but these "resident graduates" are scarcely to be considered graduate students in the modern sense. Their title suggests the provision made for them as well as their academic status: they were permitted to reside in the college community, but they received little or no attention.[10]

The *magister artium* was thus a kind of quasi-honorary designation, in which dubious condition it continued largely without change until the reformation in the 1870's when, with Harvard and Yale taking the lead, it was gradually transformed from a degree "in course" to an earned degree. However, despite the efforts of such an institution as Johns Hopkins, which in 1909 attempted to establish the master's as a degree specifically designed for college teaching, this earlier confusion has never fully been dispelled.

Since, as was said, there was no conscious differentiation in the earlier period between the institutions which remained small and single in purpose and those which have subsequently grown into larger universities providing extensive graduate study, the older colleges included in this study followed much the same pattern, playing their role in the general obfuscation. Only 18 of the 143 institutions,[11] however, offered graduate study before 1900, with another 31 "getting into the act" by 1940. Several of them, as was the case with Amherst College, were authorized to offer both bachelor's and master's degrees in their original charters.

The reformation—perhaps transition is a better term—in the degree was reflected in the report from Bucknell University: "The 'Master of Arts *in course*' had been awarded for many years—at least since 1875— to Bucknell graduates of at least three years' standing, upon application. In 1890 graduate *courses* leading to the master's degree were authorized, and apparently the practice of awarding the degree without advanced academic study ceased."

10.　Chicago: University of Chicago Press, 1953; p. 1.
11.　See footnote 1.

Wesleyan University, which had 13 students who pursued graduate study at its inception in 1890-91, changed its requirements in that latter year, on the basis of a vote of its Board of Trustees, so as to confer the master's degree upon Bachelors of Arts of Wesleyan University of at least one year's standing at the satisfactory conclusion of a course of advanced, nonprofessional study, pursued in residence for the period of not less than one year. The action further specified, "such course of study shall be under the full direction of the Committee of the Faculty on Graduate Instruction, to be composed of three permanent members with the addition of the instructor in charge of each department in which the candidate shall pursue work." Both Oberlin College and Canisius College reported similar efforts toward formalizing graduate study in the 1890's. Thus the trend in the larger institutions was paralleled in the smaller.

The early graduate programs in these colleges, moreover, were of such modest proportions that, in all likelihood, the undergraduate students were not even aware of the presence of their older confreres. The graduate program at Amherst, for example, was initiated with one student—a major in the field of mathematics. Wells College, though authorized by charter to grant advanced degrees, did not enroll its first graduate student until some years after its founding in 1868. Thus before 1900 most of these schools could boast of only a few graduate students in attendance at any one time, most of them formerly undergraduates of the same college; but the group that started graduate programs between 1900 and 1940 had much larger classes from the very beginning. In one instance the initial enrollment was as large as 51 students. In the period from 1946 to 1960, with the return of the G.I., the character of the beginning graduate programs in the small independent colleges continued to change. No longer were the graduate students enrolled in predominant numbers from the same undergraduate college—an estimated twenty-five per cent as compared with practically one hundred per cent in the earlier years. Moreover, as will be discussed later, the programs became more formal and increased in variety and complexity. What the future holds can only be guessed, but there seems little likelihood of anything but continued growth, growth in numbers, hopefully in quality, and certainly in diversity.

Since the history of graduate study in America can readily be found in a number of excellent sources,[12] this cursory review of the smaller colleges will suffice here. A more detailed treatment might tend to suggest a development on the small campus that was wholly distinct from that in the larger university. On the contrary, it is obvious that the trends in the major institutions were paralleled, perhaps unconsciously, in the liberal arts colleges.

The Rationale. Samuel Johnson was once reported to have been asked his opinion of a woman preacher who had achieved something of a vogue in contemporary London. His reply, in essence, was that the real question was not whether she was an effective preacher, but rather why she did it at all. Thus a basic question here may well be not whether these liberal arts institutions, yesterday and today, are offering effective graduate programs, but why they have entered or remained in a field which might seem more appropriate for their larger, and generally more opulent, sister institutions.

The information available on the genesis of the earlier programs is not particularly revealing, nor are the present-day directors able to offer much light on the reasons why these graduate offerings were begun. Possibly they started for much the same reason mountain climbers assail unscaled peaks—merely because the peak is there. But a brief review of the origins of the more recent programs may throw some light on the past.

Essentially, of course, the liberal arts college enters graduate study because there is a demand. Since this survey reveals that roughly seventy per cent of the candidates for master's degrees in these colleges are in the fields of elementary and secondary education, this need for professional advancement on the part of practicing or apprentice teachers would seem to represent by far the major line of force in the development of the small graduate programs.

In asking the student sample why they chose their particular gradu-

12. See, for example, Marcia Edwards, *Studies in American Graduate Education* (New York: Carnegie Foundation for the Advancement of Teaching, 1944); Byrne J. Horton, *The Graduate School, Its Origin and Administrative Development* (New York: New York University Bookstore, 1940); Will C. Ryan, *Studies in Early Graduate Education* (New York: Carnegie Foundation for the Advancement of Teaching, 1939); Richard J. Storr, *The Beginnings of Graduate Education in America* (Chicago: University of Chicago Press, 1953).

ate school, the survey elicited a variety of answers: the fact that the student wished to continue where he had had a satisfactory undergraduate experience; the desire for a small, relatively intimate academic community; the reputation of the institution for offering a quality program; the presence of a particular faculty member; the availability of a harmonious religious climate. But by far the most prevalent reason was geographical proximity to place of work or residence. A major factor in this demand, therefore, is the presence of a concentration of population and, equally, the absence of more readily available graduate opportunities from larger, more diversified, and/or less expensive institutions.

Whereas the needs of teachers comprise the principal demand for graduate study in the small college (46 colleges indicated this as the reason for instituting graduate programs), there are other needs which deserve mention. Among these are the needs of industry, which often finds itself at a competitive disadvantage in attracting personnel, particularly technical personnel, where there are no local facilities for professional advancement through academic upgrading (14 colleges established graduate programs for this purpose). Thus the origin of a number of graduate programs in small colleges lies in the active prodding from local business and industry, with the prodding often accompanied by financial and instructional support.

Another considerable segment of this demand for graduate opportunity comes from the needs of supporting religious institutions. Although only 12 colleges so indicated, the number may well be larger; for some twenty-five per cent of the 143 colleges included in this study have close church affiliation. (This point cannot be pressed too far, of course, for a high percentage of all small independent colleges and universities in the United States are church related. The directors of the study, moreover, did not consider it appropriate to ask how many of the graduate students were actively engaged in, or preparing for, service with the supporting religious body.)

This external factor of demand, however, does not provide the whole rationale for the small college engaging in graduate work. There are certain compelling internal factors as well. Among these the two strongest are undoubtedly the need to improve the attractiveness of the teaching situation and the need to obtain advanced students for specialized functions.

As for the first, any college president, dean, or departmental chairman with even brief experience with the struggle to attract good faculty in a tight market has experienced the "status" appeal of graduate instruction. This is in no way lessened by the emphasis upon research in the present pattern of doctoral study. Thus the presence or absence of graduate students and the usual concomitant of research opportunities is a significant factor in the attractiveness of a college teaching position.

And, finally, the need for more mature students for certain specialized functions has encouraged many undergraduate colleges to institute graduate offerings. Among such services the most common are those of laboratory and research assistants, apprentice instructors, and counseling or dormitory aides.

Absent from this summary of reasons for developing graduate instruction is any mention of financial incentives. And yet they deserve some attention, for, contrary to the general concept that graduate study represents an inevitable budgetary drain, there is some evidence, as will appear in a later chapter, that the opposite may be true. The least that can be said here is that few or none of the colleges in this survey gave evidence of instituting their graduate program with the conscious expectation of losing money!

Phasing In and Out. So much for the reasons why private liberal arts colleges have entered into graduate study. The manner in which they inaugurated their programs, however, is of equal interest, as is the manner in which a few of the programs, in the Tennysonian phrase, "have their day and cease to be."

In general the process for undertaking graduate programs follows a rather consistent pattern, but the total range extends from the almost accidental discovery that a student was registered for graduate work to the most careful preparation which, in one instance, extended over a period of a decade. Within these limits the information provided by the respondents would seem to justify the observation that the colleges for the most part did not engage in their new responsibilities lightly.

Although the policy in this report is to avoid identifying institutions by name, the following descriptions of program origins are identified with the approval of the institutions themselves.

The simplest of beginnings was reported by Connecticut College. In 1931-32 an instructor was accepted by the Department of History and Government as a candidate for work at the master's level and received the degree in June, 1933.

But what was acceptable in the early 1930's would scarcely be appropriate in the late '40's. Thus, in 1948, graduate study at Bennington College was begun only after the Faculty Educational Policy Committee requested each of the institution's seven divisions to make a judgment on its own capabilities for undertaking limited graduate study. One of the larger divisions responded negatively because of its feeling that the library was inadequate for advanced study in the field; another division expressed doubts about the availability of specialized equipment for either teaching or research. Initially, therefore, the graduate programs were limited to those divisions which did not require immediately a large investment in facilities or equipment. It is important to note that the divisional self-evaluations were not accepted at face value but were carefully analyzed by the committee.

The College of Saint Rose, in Albany, New York, was authorized by vote of the Board of Regents of the state to grant master's degrees on October 20, 1949, after the administration had developed a long-range program representing the culmination of a ten-year study by both faculty and administration. The plan called for immediate construction of a library building with special facilities for graduate students, and included a policy for rapidly increasing the library's holdings in reference books, periodicals, and research materials so as to support a graduate program of substantial quality. And, finally, the plan provided for the immediate addition of five full-time members of the faculty to fill any vacancies in the undergraduate instructional staff caused by siphoning off the senior persons for graduate courses.

Drury College, which entered graduate study in 1952, began by organizing a graduate council and charging it with conducting a two-year study before actual instruction would be undertaken. The principal concerns of the council were to ensure that a large enough group of qualified candidates would be available and that the new program would not "bleed" any of the energies or resources needed for successful undergraduate instruction. When the program was finally designed, the Board of Trustees guaranteed financial support for the initial year. Costs were kept reasonably low through a system of charging against the program only a minimum for overhead, thus enabling it to be virtually self-supporting from its second year of operation.

Harding College, entering the graduate field in the mid-1950's, combined so many interesting features in the development of its program that the account presented by its director is given here in full:

> From its beginning Harding College has had as one of its major goals the preparation of qualified teachers. It was this fact that prompted us to participate in the Arkansas Experiment in Teacher Education, financed by funds from the Ford Foundation. This experiment is widely known as the fifth-year program. All of the colleges in Arkansas, together with the other professional school personnel, emerged from the experiment with the strong conviction that the minimum amount of training needed to become a qualified teacher is the five-year program. At the termination of the Arkansas Experiment, the University of Arkansas was the only institution offering work for teachers beyond the four-year level. With the encouragement of the Arkansas Department of Education, Harding made plans for continuing independently the graduate program which had been developed during the co-operative experiment.
>
> A committee composed of the Director of the School of American Studies, the dean of the college, the dean of the School of American Studies, the chairman of the Department of Education, and the chairman of the Bible Department was appointed by the president and directed to study and develop a graduate program. This committee investigated all phases of the problem, including the capacity of the college to offer graduate work. Studies were made of financial resources, faculty, library facilities, classroom facilities, housing facilities, potential enrollment from teachers in the vicinity, potential enrollment from the present senior class and graduate alumni, potential enrollment from our own clientele, and potential enrollment from other four-year colleges operated by members of the Church of Christ.
>
> Graduate programs in teacher education in operation in other nearby colleges and states similar to the one finally developed by Harding were studied by the committee through visitations, correspondence, and printed literature. With the assurance that Harding could provide adequate financial support, physical facilities, and faculty the committee designed and recommended the program which was approved by the faculty and board of trustees early in 1955 and placed in operation during the 1955-56 school year.

A somewhat different approach was taken by Hollins College in developing its program in 1958-59. In this instance the departments concerned—first psychology, then later English and modern languages —drew up careful blueprints of the types of programs which they wished to offer. These were submitted to specialists in the field as well as to departments in other institutions providing similar study. The outsiders were requested to comment both upon the quality of the program and upon the competence of the personnel who would participate in offering it. Since the responses were favorable, the plan was then submitted to the Board of Trustees of the college, which approved its adoption.

Manhattanville College of the Sacred Heart (1948-49) used a variation of this approach by establishing an *ad hoc* advisory committee comprised of such outstanding educational statesmen as Frank Bowles, Roy J. Deferrari, Frank D. Fackenthal, George W. McClelland, Edward Rooney, S.J., Guy E. Snavely, William P. Tolley, and Levering Tyson.

Since one of the principal problems in developing any graduate program is to ascertain the potential supply of capable graduate students, the University of Scranton, through the office of its registrar, made a survey of graduates and teachers in the area of northeastern Pennsylvania. As a result, it estimated that some four hundred persons would be interested initially in graduate instruction and that there would be a sufficient annual supply of new students to justify the development of a program in education. Finally, local school superintendents and representatives of the state Department of Public Instruction were consulted on the need and advisability of the proposed endeavor.

This accounting could be substantially extended, of course. The brief descriptions of the origins of graduate programs in this highly selected group of institutions, however, reveal the general outlines followed in a great many of the programs. Although in a few instances administrations appeared to have carried the major brunt of development, the graduate programs were normally evolved by means of studies conducted by faculty committees in conjunction with the administration. In a few instances the studies appeared to extend over only a few months. For the most part, however, at least a year was spent before plans were submitted to the faculty for adoption, and from the faculty to the board of trustees.

But what of the experiences of colleges in discontinuing graduate study, once it has started? Unfortunately the statute of limitations adopted for institutional inclusion in this phase of the study does not permit much information about the decline and fall of graduate programs in the small college, for there have been very few casualties since 1950—a period of academic inflation. Nevertheless, two colleges which were in the graduate business for some years either drastically curtailed or completely eliminated their programs during this period. While for purposes of propriety these institutions are not identified here, the following reports may be of interest:

> **College A.** Our master's degree program was never very extensive in terms of student numbers and/or areas covered. Rather than being discontinued I should say that it faded away by lack of administration approval. I am sure there are a few faculty people who would like to get back into business again. My objection to such a program is that it becomes necessarily third rate—for under the pressure of adequate staff, such as existing at the present time, master's degree work must necessarily be imposed on existing faculty loads. This is hard to justify for a small enrollment which consists primarily of young instructors. . . . Curiously enough, our catalogue still makes mention of the program, as follows: "The College may confer the degree of Master of Arts on students who satisfy the requirements for this degree." I suppose this is done in case we should ever wish formally to reinstate it.[13]

> **College B.** This college is discontinuing its graduate program. Its work in psychology, in special education, and in physical education ends with the current academic year. Its work in education will continue two years after this year. Some of the questions which you ask, for example about budget, were central questions in the decision to discontinue the work. We felt that much more budget must be put into the graduate program if it were to be continued.[14]

Thus master's degree programs in the private colleges come, and a few of them go. Although representing only a small fraction of the total graduate study in the United States, the efforts of these smaller institutions are not inconsiderable. Moreover, they are rapidly expanding, as nearly all segments of business, industry, government, and education seek persons with more advanced and specialized training.

In the succeeding chapters of this study, therefore, an effort has

13. Letter dated December 27, 1961.
14. Letter dated December 14, 1961.

been made to provide a detailed description of these programs, showing their dimensions, their functions, their problems, and aspirations. From the resultant portrait it is hoped that those in charge of present programs may find an improved measure for self-evaluation. Further, some colleges now capable of inaugurating graduate programs of high calibre may be encouraged to do so. Negatively, some of the less well-equipped colleges which may now be contemplating graduate study may be discouraged therefrom.

If these are the only results, however, the study will have failed to accomplish one of its major aims. For, as discussed earlier, the whole praxis of master's study is badly in need of a new, more creative impulse. The larger, more well-established, more "traditional" graduate schools do not seem to be providing this impulse, possibly because their primary interest is in the doctorate. But is it too much to hope that the newer, smaller graduate schools, in colleges relatively independent of fixed public demands, may be encouraged singly or jointly to evolve fresh blueprints for graduate study which may resuscitate the master's degree and help it fulfill a genuine and mounting public need?

CHAPTER II

Authorization and Accreditation

The brief review of the genesis of graduate work in the private liberal arts colleges given in Chapter I suggests that a high percentage of the programs during the earlier years of this development were not concerned with any external controls which might be exercised by regional, state, or professional agencies. However, the rapid growth of graduate study in recent years, which parallels the rapid growth of formal accreditation,[1] is adding a new dimension to the problem of external control. Dean Walter F. Loehwing, of the State University of Iowa, while president of the Association of Graduate Schools, gave expression to this developing concern as follows:

> Great pressures for accreditation of graduate schools exist because of the recent establishment of graduate schools in many institutions which cannot offer either well-rounded or high-quality programs. The formation, by American universities, of the National Commission on Accrediting and the recent interest of the North Central Association of [sic] Teacher Training Programs at the graduate level suggests that some organization will soon formally undertake accreditation of graduate schools.[2]

1. For an excellent review of this development see William K. Selden, *Accreditation: A Struggle Over Standards in Higher Education* (New York: Harper & Brothers, 1960).
2. In "Report of the Executive Committee," *Journal of Proceedings and Addresses of the Sixtieth Annual Conference (AAU) and the Eleventh Annual Conference (AGS) (New York: October 27-28, 1959)*, p. 18. For a discus-

Although the association subsequently voted that it would not itself undertake responsibility for accreditation of graduate programs, leaving this function to other agencies, its continued concern is nevertheless a matter of record.

Since at least 70 of the independent liberal arts colleges have indicated an intention of getting on the graduate-school bandwagon, it seemed desirable in this study to ascertain what, if any, requirements and/or recommendations the already established accrediting agencies or associations may have devised for the control of master's study. To obtain this information an inquiry was addressed to all of the regional accrediting associations, all of the state departments of education, and to 196 professional groups selected from the 1960-61 directory of educational associations published by the United States Office of Education. The returns showed a very active interest, but little in the way of specific regulation of programs leading to the master's degree. There are, however, noticeable trends in that direction on the part of all of the regional associations, some of the state departments of education, and a few of the professional organizations. Moreover, the "inspector general" of accrediting agencies, the National Commission on Accrediting, has only recently established a committee to study the problem of accrediting graduate study on all levels.

The general policy of the six regional associations is not to accredit graduate study as such but to consider it a part of the total institutional program. In the words of Dr. F. Taylor Jones, executive secretary of the Middle States Association's Commission on Institutions of Higher Education, "With us, it is all or nothing in all cases."[3] Nevertheless, the Middle States Association has published a list of criteria for the self-evaluation of graduate programs, in which the basic philosophy is phrased as follows:

> An educational institution's usefulness to society is determined more by the excellence than by the diversity of its services. It should therefore limit its commitments to the areas in which it can provide superior performance. Graduate work of high quality lays so heavy a demand upon staff, facilities, and administration that only the

---

sion of the experiences of the Association of American Universities in the field of accreditation see William K. Selden, "The Judgment Seat: The AAU and Accreditation," in *Graduate Journal* II (Fall, 1959), pp. 325-33.

3. Letter dated September 19, 1960.

strongest institutions should undertake it, and they should do so in only their best fields. Other institutions will serve better by concentrating on programs for which their resources are clearly adequate.[4]

The North Central Association of Colleges and Secondary Schools, which has within recent years made substantial changes in its accreditation procedures, takes cognizance of any new graduate program in accordance with the following procedure:

> Under the current policies (January, 1959) of the Commission on Colleges and Universities of the North Central Association, accredited higher institutions come under review when they move from undergraduate education to the offering of graduate programs or from one graduate level to another.[5]

For some years the association has followed well-defined policies in accrediting graduate programs in education. More recently, moreover, it has established a Committee on Graduate Degrees which has for its responsibility "the development of procedures specifically for the evaluation of graduate programs."[6]

The same procedure is under consideration by the Southern Association of Colleges and Secondary Schools as well. Gordon Sweet, the executive secretary of the association, wrote on September 23, 1960:

> The Southern Association does not investigate or accredit graduate programs separately from a study or accreditation of the college or university as a whole. We have been concerned recently, however, about member colleges, which have not had graduate programs, moving rather suddenly into a graduate program. In many cases it has been into one area only, that of education. The Council of the Commission has, therefore, established the policy stated below:
>
> "That a Senior College planning to offer graduate degrees (moving to a higher degree level) should notify the Executive Secretary's office immediately of its intention, and give evidence that it is legally authorized to do so by charter. Such a college is encouraged to complete the Institutional Self-Study and Periodic Visitation Program before

4. "Graduate Work," Commission on Institutions of Higher Education, Middle States Association of Colleges and Secondary Schools. Document No. 4.72 (May, 1959). See Appendix IV.
5. *North Central Association Quarterly* XXXIII (January, 1959), p. 1.
6. Letter from Norman Burns, secretary of the association, dated September 30, 1960. Also, see Appendix IV.

offering graduate degrees and must be subject to a special report and possibly a visitation by a Commission committee."[7]

Thus, all of the six regional associations, as stated previously, have expressed an active concern with the rapid expansion of graduate programs—the Northwest Association, for example, has a special committee to make studies and policy recommendations—and most of them have published more or less detailed guideposts for institutional self-evaluation on this level (reproduced in part in Appendix IV). As the expansion continues, one can predict with reasonable assurance that these associations will feel a greater and greater responsibility to introduce new forms of control.

The same prediction would probably hold good for supervision by state departments of education, which have already, of course, evolved a fairly high degree of control over certain professional areas. In describing the present status of state accreditation Theresa Birch Wilkins wrote as follows:

> Diversity characterizes the pattern of accrediting responsibility assumed by agencies within the States. Although in seven States no agency on the State level is reported as engaging in accrediting, actually in only two States—New Mexico and North Dakota—and the territory of Hawaii is there no agency responsible for some form of institutional approval.
>
> The areas in which State agencies accredit are primarily: teacher education, general college status, and junior college status. The State department of education assumes major responsibility for accrediting institutions and programs for teacher education. . . .
>
> Dependence on private voluntary accrediting agencies is evidenced in many States. A number of State agencies reported that they either accept the accreditation of a regional or nation-wide agency as a basis for their own approval for specific purposes or use the criteria developed by these agencies with necessary modifications to suit local conditions.[8]

It should be noted that Mrs. Wilkins is silent on the accreditation of graduate work as such. By and large state control at this level seems to have been exercised traditionally through the institutional charter.

7. Letter dated September 23, 1960. Also, see Appendix IV.
8. Theresa Wilkins, "Accreditation in the States," in *Accreditation in Higher Education*, ed. Lloyd E. Blauch (Washington: United States Government Printing Office, 1959), p. 41.

Relatively few of the colleges in the survey, however, indicated any particular difficulty in obtaining charter revision, if such revision was indeed necessary. The older institutions seem generally to have been granted such broad charters as to permit them to offer nearly any degree current in either American or European universities.

The second traditional way of state accreditation is through controlling certification requirements; but in practice this represents not so much an effort at "quality control" as an insistence on the provision of certain specific courses. As for the more recent trends in state accreditation, the evidence points to an increasing reliance upon the regional or professional accrediting agencies, frequently with a representative of the state department of education serving as a member of accrediting teams. New York State, on the other hand, is in the process of developing its own criteria for evaluating graduate study. A preliminary draft of these criteria is reproduced at the end of Appendix IV.

In Appendix III are given lists of the professional agencies which are recognized as having accrediting functions by either the U. S. Office of Education or the National Commission on Accrediting.[9] On the whole these agencies are not directly concerned with the types of graduate programs generally found in the private, independently structured college. Even where there may be some interest, the official stand of the organization is usually similar to that expressed by Frank Verblugge, secretary of the American Association of Physics Teachers:

> The American Association of Physics Teachers has by design stayed clear of any effort to certify programs for physics majors either at the undergraduate or graduate level. . . . Requirements for a major in physics, both at the undergraduate and at the graduate level, are the responsibility of the individual college or university. A majority of academic physicists are of the opinion that this is the desirable situation and one which we should continue to encourage.[10]

Even the American Chemical Society, which lays down the most stringent requirements for the accreditation of undergraduate majors, has not as yet included graduate study in its evaluative process, partly, one understands, because it has not fully resolved the questions of just how and what to evaluate.

9.   Pp. 155-56.
10.   Letter dated May 24, 1960.

On the other hand, the American Library Association has been accrediting training programs for librarianship since 1953, following the adoption of its "Standards for Accreditation" in July of 1951. Under these standards, which apply to the basic five-year program beyond the secondary school and leading normally to the master's degree, 32 institutions had been accredited by the close of 1960.[11]

Since, as has been indicated earlier, many of the graduate programs in the colleges included in this survey are occupied with teacher education, it is important here to observe that in this particular area the agencies for external control are both present and vigorous. In addition to the state departments of education, which exercise control as part of licensing or certification procedures, the National Council for Accreditation of Teacher Education is making a strong bid for acceptance as the accrediting agency in this professional area. Already 27 of the state departments of education have given some degree of official recognition to NCATE accreditation. It must be said, nevertheless, that widespread dissatisfaction with the policies and practices of NCATE has been voiced. Dr. William K. Selden, in his recent article entitled "Basic Issues in Accreditation of Teacher Education," describes the problem as follows:

> Almost no activity in higher education is more widely misunderstood or subjected to such diverse criticisms as accreditation. Especially is this the case with respect to accreditation in teacher education, a field of study about which many educators regardless of academic background will often speak with more passion than judgment. It is difficult to bring clarity into discussions on this subject because almost every comment, no matter how diverse or extreme, is based upon some element of truth though rarely do comments take into account all of the factors involved.[12]

11. As of the date of writing this chapter, studies are reportedly under way for defining the content of graduate training programs for sociologists, political scientists, biologists, and mathematicians, among others. These presumably will result in recommended standards rather than in formal accrediting procedures. The American Personnel and Guidance Association, through its Committee on Professional Training, Licensing and Certification, published in October, 1958, recommended minimum standards for the master's degree in its field. Similarly the American Society for Engineering Education has sponsored several reports on effective graduate study in engineering. See also, *Graduate Education in Psychology*, ed. Anne Roe (Washington: American Psychological Association, 1959).

12. *Liberal Education* XLVII (December, 1961), pp. 536-46.

The resolution of this conflict, which must come in the near future, will undoubtedly have an impact upon the accreditation of teacher education programs on both the undergraduate and graduate levels. In the meantime it would be incumbent upon the small college considering the development of a graduate program in this field to make itself *au courant* with the forces and counterforces in this academic debate. This is particularly true because of the present quantitative requirements for NCATE accreditation.

This survey of external controls indicates that there are relatively few regional, public, or professional associations which appear to be occupied with accrediting graduate study as such. This is not to say that these agencies are disinterested. On the contrary, there is ample evidence that at least the regional associations look very critically at graduate study both in terms of its inherent quality and of its possible impact upon the more traditional functions of the college. It is almost redundant to say that there is still need for a more vigorous effort to enforce high standards of performance at the master's level, whether in the small college or in the large university. Toward that end, as indicated previously, the National Commission on Accrediting has only recently established a committee to study the problem of graduate standards, and the newly formed Council of Graduate Schools in the United States has adopted as one of its objectives "the improvement and advancement of graduate education." The constitution of this latter organization goes on to say that "the purview of the Council includes all matters germane to this purpose."[13]

In the meantime the colleges have relied largely upon their own resources in evaluating their capacity for offering graduate study. To what extent this will be shortly supplemented by formal accrediting procedures remains to be seen. "The great question in accrediting graduate work," according to Dr. Selden, "is how it should be evaluated and on what basis, especially since the relationship of the individual professor to the individual student is by far the most important factor."[14]

13. Brochure entitled *The Council of Graduate Schools in the United States* (September, 1961).
14. Letter dated November 22, 1961.

CHAPTER III

Administrative Considerations

Although it would be something of an overstatement to assert that the graduate divisions in the American colleges and universities are disorganized, they have not developed, even in the larger institutions, nearly so much centralized control as have undergraduate or the more highly articulated professional schools.[1] There are certain endemic reasons for this lack of development. Essentially, of course, graduate study tends to be highly individualized. Thus the departmental structure which, often not without a struggle, has been brought or held under control at the undergraduate level, tends to occupy a place of paramount importance in the graduate school administration. It may be, too, that the development of most graduate programs as extensions of undergraduate offerings has resulted in a kind of deferred maturity in their organization. Thus many graduate school deans, even in some of the larger programs, exercise very little control or centralized direction, but serve, rather, a quasi-secretarial function.

1. Morris A. Stewart, in "The Organization of the Graduate School," makes the following observation: "There is less uniformity of organization among graduate schools in the United States than there is among undergraduate colleges. This is, perhaps, inevitable, and it is advantageous in many ways. However, if the differences become too great, advanced degrees will ultimately lose all meaning."—*Journal of Higher Education* XXX (March, 1959), pp. 136-37.

From this study of the smaller colleges it would appear almost as if the lack of strong central control in the graduate program was by deliberation rather than by chance. For nearly every person with whom the investigators consulted laid great emphasis upon the institution's desire to keep the undergraduate function in the forefront as the predominant and most important interest—a balance which tends to discourage a strong or aggressive graduate administration.

Faculty members as well as presidents and deans in a large majority of the colleges expressed concern lest the graduate program should in any manner interfere with the progress of the undergraduate college. To carry this a step further, many persons indicated that the main reason for instituting graduate instruction was to strengthen the undergraduate resources, both human and physical, and perhaps even spiritual. In the best relationship, therefore, the two programs are integrated, but with the higher program used as a stimulus and supplement to the lower.

Thus it was not a surprise, on our inquiring who was in charge of the graduate program, to receive answers which ranged from "no one" to "president of the college." Moreover, there are few definitive patterns traceable to the type of graduate program which the institution maintains. Generally speaking, where the graduate work is exclusively designed for the training of elementary—or secondary—school teachers, the officer in charge is the head of the undergraduate program in education. Generally speaking, too, where the program is designed almost exclusively to meet the interests of some local industry, the officer in charge is the departmental chairman, usually in the sciences, who best understands the requirements of the industrial sponsors. Similarly, the experimental programs—and these are few indeed—may come under the supervision of the individual who conceived them. But as will be seen in Table 1, the central direction of the graduate program varies widely.

But these by no means cover the full range. In other colleges the direction of the graduate program is assigned to such officers as the executive vice president (3), the registrar (1), the director of admissions (2), the director of the fifth-year program (1), a member of the executive committee (1), and so forth.

Since administration of the graduate program seems in only a minority of the colleges to represent a full-time assignment—an esti-

TABLE 1

Administrative Titles of Directors of Graduate Programs

Number of Colleges

Director of the Graduate Program	29
Chairman of the Committee on Graduate Study	28
Dean of the Graduate Program	26
Dean of the College	24
President of the College	8
Secretary of the Graduate Council	7
Chairman of the Graduate Division	6

mated 14 out of the 143 programs have a full-time officer in charge—a side glance was given to the undergraduate title of the person responsible for the program. Fifty-eight of the institutions assigned the advanced program to that workhorse of the campus, the academic dean or academic vice president. The other principal officer was the departmental chairman; and here the range of subject fields covered nearly the entire undergraduate curriculum, with education taking the lead. It is interesting that in eight colleges the president himself assumes direct responsibility for advanced study. That he has enough time free from fund raising and housekeeping to undertake such an academic responsibility is pleasant to contemplate.

It would seem, therefore, that insofar as over-all direction of the graduate program is concerned, the operating principle is the same as that which dominates so much of academic administration. That is, the important consideration is the man rather than the title. This was borne out in the campus visits where, in response to an inquiry as to the reason the particular director was selected, the following considerations were most generally offered: interest in the program, ability to cooperate with administration and faculty, initiative in assuming responsibility, availability, and willingness to add something new to an already heavy load of administrative or academic responsibilities. Very few of the colleges sought a person from an external source to head up the graduate program—in one instance the dean emeritus stayed around to do it—and very few colleges considered the direction of the graduate program a full-time assignment. Moreover, in a number of colleges, the responsibility was assigned not to a single individual but rather to a group, with or without some such specific designation as the "graduate study committee."

Certainly one of the most important responsibilities of the director of any academic program is planning and coordinating the curriculum. It might be expected, therefore, that whenever the colleges designated an officer to supervise the graduate program, this would be among his major responsibilities. It was, in approximately 35 of the colleges. Nevertheless, as is evident from Table 2, curricular planning is more generally viewed as a joint responsibility. Thus, some of the institutions utilize the entire faculty; others—and these constitute a substantial percentage of the total—use the graduate council or another form of committee to carry out this assignment.

TABLE 2

Officer or Group Responsible for Curriculum Planning *

Number of Colleges

Graduate Council	79
Departmental Chairmen	38
Faculty	25
Director of the Graduate Program	19
Curriculum Committee	18
Academic Dean	12
Academic Senate	4
Graduate Faculty	3
Faculty Administrative Committee	2
Committee on Instruction	2
Graduate Department of Education	2
Division Director and his Advisory Committee	1
Coordinated Colleges Committee	1
Trustees	1

Forty-one of the colleges assign the organization and administration of the curriculum to two different groups or administrators; ten colleges to three groups; one college to four groups.

It is obvious from Table 2 that the faculty feels a keen responsibility for the graduate program, a fact which was consistently borne out in the campus interviews. Generally, the proposal for a graduate course originates at the departmental level on the basis of a felt need (or aggressive insistence of a member of the department or its chairman). It then goes usually to a committee of the faculty, which accepts, modifies, or rejects it. Moreover, the impression seems to be that these proposals are much more often accepted than rejected. The time-honored system of logrolling may well have originated in the groves of academe! Nevertheless, the feeling elicited in the interviews was very strongly in favor of a responsible graduate faculty in matters of curriculum development.

Since one of the most essential administrative tasks in any academic organization is admission, and since here too there is a rather wide range of patterns in the larger graduate schools, it is not surprising that the same range of possibilities exists in the smaller colleges as well.

TABLE 3

Officer or Group Responsible in Admission *

Number of Colleges

Graduate Council	49
Director of the Graduate Program	48
Chairman of the Department Concerned	41
Admissions Office	29
Academic Dean	13
Registrar	10
Faculty Committee	9
Chairman, Department of Education	3
Director of Community Education	1
Representative of Faculty	1
Chairman, Graduate Council	1
Coordinator of College Administration	1
Director of Evening Division	1
Assistant to the Dean	1
Provost	1
Committee on Fifth Year	1
Associate Dean of the College	1
Committee of Field Coordinators	1
Director of Summer School	1
Director, Center for Liberal Studies in Education	1
Faculty at Large	1

*Admission of graduate students was the responsibility of three different officers in eight colleges; two officers in 56 colleges; one officer in the remaining colleges.

Evidently the only person who does not in some way get into the act is the president of the college, despite the fact that on some campuses he directs the total program. The heavy emphasis on what might be considered group responsibility suggests a conscious effort to maintain a degree of uniformity in admission standards. In a number of instances, even where there is no such committee responsibility, the responses indicate that two and sometimes three officers share responsibility for admissions. (This, for the mathematically inclined, explains why the totals in Table 3 are somewhat in excess of the number of colleges involved in this study.)

General examinations are provided in many of the colleges in this group for purposes of determining admission, candidacy, and graduation. In a few instances the colleges use such nationally standardized tests as the Graduate Record Examinations for these purposes. A majority, however, seem to assume responsibility for developing their own examinations, either written or oral, at least for purposes other than admission. The assignment of responsibility for such examinations, particularly the examinations for candidacy or graduation, breaks down as shown in Table 4.

TABLE 4

Officer or Group Responsible for General Examinations

	Number of Colleges
Departmental Chairmen	53
Graduate Council	31
Director of the Graduate Program	22
Faculty	12
Academic Dean	6
The Student's Advisory Committee	6
Department of Education	6
Director of Testing	5
Graduate Study Committee	4
Divisional Chairman	2
Assistant to the Dean	2
Graduate Instructors	2
Registrar	2
Dean of Students	1
Guidance Director	1
Director of Summer School	1

As one expects, student records are maintained in the office of the registrar in a considerable majority of the colleges (112 out of 143). The surprising thing is that 37 of the colleges seem to have worked out a variant system of keeping records of the graduate students. The replies to the questionnaires indicate that in some of the institutions the task is assigned to two administrators or groups and in some others to three persons. As Table 5 shows, where a college places its graduate program under a graduate dean, there seems to be a tendency to assign student records to his direct supervision.

TABLE 5

Officer or Group Responsible for Keeping Records

Number of Colleges

Registrar	112
Dean of Graduate Study	30
Departmental Chairmen	8
Academic Dean	7
Secretary of Graduate Studies	6
Committee on Graduate Study	3
Clerk	1
Student Personnel Office	1
Committee on Advanced Degrees	1
Director of the Evening Division	1
Director of Community Education	1
Chairman, Department of Education and Psychology	1
Assistant to the Dean	1
Assistant Director of Graduate Study	1
Education Office	1
Graduate Office	1
Provost	1
Division for Counseling	1
Minor Field Advisers	1

Except where graduate courses are totally separate from the undergraduate, the scheduling of the courses and the assignment of rooms must obviously be coordinated with the total program of the college. At one of the reporting institutions the task is easy. There is no scheduling officer because there are no formal classes in the graduate program. For the most part, though, this task is a relatively important one in the total administrative function; and, despite the fact that it would appear to call for a highly individual approach, a surprising number of the institutions, as is evident from Table 6, seem to consider it something of a group responsibility.

TABLE 6

Officer or Group Responsible for Scheduling

Number of Colleges

Departmental Chairman	41
Dean of the Graduate Program	41
Registrar	30
Academic Dean	27
Committee on Graduate Study	15
Faculty Committee	5
Faculty Adviser	2
Assistant to the Dean	2
Secretary of Graduate Studies	2
Divisional Chairman	2
Student Personnel Office	1
Director, Division of Community Education	1
Department of Education	1
Schedule Officer	1
Catalogue Committee	1
College Extension Officer	1
Faculty	1
Director of Teacher Education	1
Associate Dean of the College	1
Academic Vice President	1

One of the most difficult areas in the entire study, as will be evident in Chapter VII, has to do with finances. (Except for revising a curriculum, this is one of the most difficult areas in all of higher education!) A particular complication in determining responsibility for the graduate school budget in the small college is the lack of clear delineation between the undergraduate and graduate schools' financial structure. In a number of instances this duality has necessitated direct representation from both levels. Forty-eight colleges indicate that two administrators are responsible for the graduate budget; nine colleges, that three are involved; and three colleges, that four officers are assigned to this responsibility. The very complexity of the problem undoubtedly made a simple and direct answer to this portion of the survey questionnaire rather difficult, and thus Table 7 can do no more than suggest the wide range of solutions to the problem of budgetary supervision.

TABLE 7

Officer or Group Responsible for the Budget

Number of Colleges

Business Manager, Treasurer, Comptroller, or Bursar	50
President	49
Director of Graduate Study	38
Departmental Chairman	25
Academic Dean	19
Committee on Graduate Study	8
Budget Committee or Finance Committee	8
Vice President	5
Administrative Group	5
Board of Trustees	4
Chairman of Division	2
Administrative Director	1
Provost	1
Director of Teacher Education	1
Director of Community Education	1
Director of Summer School	1

The task of assigning classrooms may not be on the same level of administrative complexity as that of designing and maintaining the budget. Nevertheless, as anyone who has ever had to struggle with this annual chess game knows, it can at times be a most harassing task. Because of the necessity of careful coordination between the undergraduate and graduate courses, it is natural that the responsible officer in carrying out this function in most of the institutions is either the registrar (54), the academic dean (36), or the director of the graduate program (23).

Counseling is evidently recognized as a proper responsibility by most of the colleges in the survey. It is also, rightly, a shared responsibility, with 45 of these institutions indicating that it is shared by two officers or groups and five others indicating either three officers or committees. But because of the highly individual nature of graduate study the person most intimately concerned with counseling, as is evident in Table 8, is inevitably the departmental chairman. Where the college has available one or more specialists in areas of non-academic counseling, the table suggests that the graduate students have access to these individuals as well.

TABLE 8

Officer or Group Responsible for Counseling

Number of Colleges

Departmental Chairmen	62
Director of the Graduate Program	48
Faculty Advisers	27
Academic Dean	15
Faculty Committee	5
Student Personnel Office	5
Counseling Center	5
Dean of Students	5
Graduate Council	5
Chairman of a Division	5
Department of Education	4
Chairman, Graduate Council	2
College Psychologist	1
Chaplain	1
Director of Guidance	1
Director of Summer School	1
Associate Dean of the College	1
Assistant to the Dean	1
Department of Religion	1
Director of Community Education	1
Director of Teacher Education	1
Field Coordinator	1

Because many of the larger graduate schools have in recent years come to recognize the need for some type of directed social activity for their graduate students and have even, in a number of instances, provided full-time personnel to look after this need, it is interesting to note that the area of social activity receives relatively little attention in the group of institutions in this survey. The reasons for this are not difficult to adduce. Many of the programs are small, scheduled in the late afternoon and evening, and peopled by individuals who are engaged in full-time employment and whose social interests are already established in their local community. One respondent asserted that the intellectual atmosphere in the graduate program was so "rarified" that there was little if any need for a formalized social program. That the social requirements of the graduate students are not totally overlooked, however, is suggested by Table 9.

TABLE 9

Officer or Group Responsible for the Conduct of Social Activity

	Number of Colleges
Dean of Students	33
Director of Graduate Study	13
Student Committee	8
Faculty Committee	7
Departmental Chairmen	6
Academic Dean	5
Committee on Graduate Study	3
Social Committee	2
Director of Residence	1
Graduate Council Representative	1
Moderator of Graduate Students Organization	1
Junior Faculty Members	1
Faculty	1
Graduate Club	1
Jointly with College	1

It should be noted in passing that increasing attention is being paid to this phase of the graduate programs in the liberal arts colleges. In discussions with the deans, it appeared that they feel the present dropout rate might be reduced if the graduate student could develop a greater sense of identity with the school. Moreover, they believe an organized approach to the problem would better create a true "community of scholars," in which the graduate student would have an opportunity on the smaller campus, somewhat comparable with that on the larger, for stimulation and cross-fertilization. Thus there is a beginning trend toward providing both counseling and social activity along lines similar to those which are now deemed essential in undergraduate programs.

Placement service in the graduate programs was not particularly bothersome because many graduate students in the private colleges are already engaged in vocational pursuits. Many of the other students are studying in such areas as science or business administration, where the demand for highly trained personnel does not suggest the need for any intensified placement activity on the part of the college. However, the majority of the colleges do recognize some responsibility in this area. In 67 institutions the placement office is available to graduate as well as undergraduate students. In another 30, the departmental chairmen are listed as responsible for assisting the master's candidate in securing employment. In another four the director of teacher placement is the responsible officer.

General Observations. Whereas in many of the colleges surveyed the administrative structure of the graduate school is merely an extension of the undergraduate, it is evident from the total survey that a wider variety of patterns exists on the graduate level. The determining factors would appear to be the nature and objectives of the program and the capabilities and interests of the individuals concerned. There is little effort to provide a totally separate administration for the graduate programs, in part because they are small, in part because of the desire, emphasized on nearly every campus, to ensure that the advanced work will supplement and not impede the basic function of the institution—that is, the baccalaureate program. Separate administrations were evident principally in those schools where the graduate offerings are limited to one specific field, such as education, or where they are offered only in the summertime. In both these instances the work bears little immediate relevance to the primary operations of the institution.

It would be interesting to see if the administrative structure of the graduate program has any relation to the over-all quality of performance. Unfortunately, the scope of this study made any such qualitative observations impossible. The investigators were interested to note, however, one possible trend in developing administrative structures which may ultimately have some bearing upon quality. Whereas the origin of many of the graduate programs seemed to be in one or two departments, with an aggressive departmental chairman successfully promoting the idea among his faculty colleagues, there is some evidence that the college president himself is beginning more and more to be concerned with the integrity of the graduate offerings. That is not to suggest that the graduate programs would be improved if they were directly supervised by the president. In view of the many other demands on his time, the opposite might well occur. Nevertheless, in a number of colleges, possibly because of the expansion of the graduate program, of the increased interest on the part of foundations in the development of graduate study, and of the wide demands for persons with graduate training, the presidents seem to be becoming increasingly interested in strong and creative administrative nurture for this offshoot from the main stem of the institutional structure.

CHAPTER IV

The Graduate Faculty

A perspicacious college president once observed that as long as an institution had a good chef it could afford to get along with a rather indifferent faculty. Despite the garden variety of wisdom in this observation, its applicability to the graduate programs in the independent college would appear to be rather limited. For the major concern voiced by faculty and administration alike, in their responses to this survey, seems to be that of obtaining and retaining a core of graduate teachers capable of affecting eternity, which, according to Henry Adams, is both the teacher's mission and opportunity. It is the purpose of this chapter, therefore, to examine the status of the graduate faculty in the liberal arts college.

Looking first at the source of instructional personnel—and we are dealing with approximately 2,500 faculty members—it is gratifying to note that close to ninety per cent of them are drawn from the full-time teaching staffs, with nearly all of this group engaged in instructing both undergraduate and graduate students.[1] Only three colleges, in fact, stated that all of their full-time graduate faculty taught graduate courses only. Thus it can be said—and this is presented with no great air of discovery—that the primary source for the full-time graduate faculty in the private college is the undergraduate teaching staff.

1. Four colleges indicated that they had no graduate faculty as such, since all the graduate work was organized on a tutorial basis.

It can further be said that an outstanding characteristic of graduate programs in the independently structured colleges is their combining undergraduate and graduate instruction in teaching assignments. Only 49 of the 143 institutions indicated that they had any faculty members teaching graduate courses only; and it can be assumed that a substantial percentage in this category were outside specialists engaged to give one or two advanced courses.

Unfortunately the scope of the questionnaire did not permit any evaluation of the force of graduate study in attracting new full-time faculty members. There is ample evidence, however, both from the campus visits and the survey of faculty opinion to indicate that this is indeed a prime consideration. Thus, although undergraduate faculty can be considered the major source for graduate faculty, the presence of a graduate program is a factor in attracting teachers to the institution in the first place.

Seventy-seven of the colleges surveyed indicated that they used part-time faculty members—to a total of 418—who were concerned with graduate courses. The origins of these part-time personnel are quite varied. Thirty-five colleges stated that they drew on nearby colleges and universities, and another 35 colleges (an unexpectedly small figure) found part-time faculty in the neighboring public schools. This figure may actually be somewhat larger inasmuch as another 17 stated that they used outside specialists, with the field undesignated. That only eight employed men from industry as members of the graduate faculty suggests, especially for those colleges situated in areas of high industrial concentration, that here is a largely untapped source of supply. Other sources of part-time faculty members comprise such diverse areas as the religious community, local research institutes, state departments of education, Y.M.C.A.'s, public library systems, military installations, private day schools, and so forth. It is quite evident, therefore, that the colleges have had to exercise a degree of ingenuity in discovering competent personnel to supplement their own faculty resources in the conduct of graduate programs. The strong preference for utilizing the institution's own full-time staff is explained by some of the respondents in terms of the degree of control which can be exercised over quality of instruction. The outsider may very often bring a wealth of experience to the classroom, but he is not likely to feel the same sense of identification with the institution or to respond quite so favorably to suggestions from the director of the program.

Figures 1A and 1B provide a graphic indication of the assignment of teaching staff in the graduate programs.

FIGURE 1A

Number of Colleges Employing Faculty Members Exclusively in a Graduate Teaching Capacity Compared with the Number of Colleges Employing Teachers for Both Graduate and Undergraduate Teaching

(Data Based on Questionnaire "B")

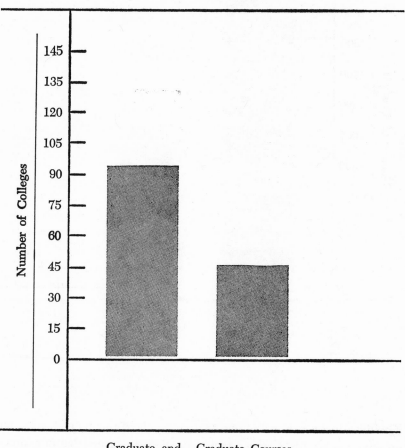

Graduate and Undergraduate   Graduate Courses Only

Frequency of Faculty Members Teaching in the Graduate Program Exclusively Compared with Those Teaching Both Graduate and Undergraduate Courses

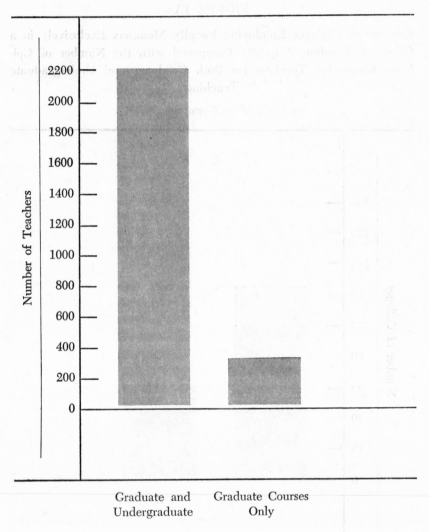

Graduate and
Undergraduate

Graduate Courses
Only

Qualifications. A primary consideration of the directors of the various graduate programs, commendably enough, is to ensure that only qualified faculty members teach graduate courses. Of the 143 colleges in this study, seven stated unequivocally that the graduate faculty must possess the doctorate. Forty-four provided an escape clause by insisting on the doctorate or its equivalent in specialized experience. This experience, as specified by a few respondents, included demonstrable accomplishments in research. Nearly all of the colleges required at least the master's degree or a terminal degree in the area of specialization; and a substantial number indicated that they looked for extensive and effective teaching experience before assignment to graduate courses.

A determining factor in assigning graduate courses is demonstrable competence in teaching advanced undergraduate courses. The significance of this lies, in part, in the fact that a considerable number of the graduate courses in the smaller colleges are combined with more advanced undergraduate offerings.

In establishing requirements for the graduate faculty, at least one college specifies that no department may have more than one person without a doctorate teaching graduate courses. This may imply a movement in the direction of the team approach, frequently propounded in discussions of the utilization of graduate resources. There is no indication, however, that this device has had a favorable reception in smaller institutions, possibly because it is potentially more expensive than assignment of the single instructor per course.

Finally, one of the important qualifications in the selection of graduate faculty, as stressed by a number of the respondents, is interest in graduate teaching. There is by no means unanimity of opinion on the campuses of the colleges surveyed concerning the desirability of maintaining graduate programs. Faculty members who are vigorously opposed to the idea, despite their other abilities, are generally not asked to participate.

Teaching Load. Despite the practice in many of the larger graduate schools of providing the instructor with extra "credit" for graduate courses—for example, four hours of teaching credit for a three-hour course—75 of the 143 colleges indicated that they make no distinction between graduate and undergraduate courses in computing the faculty members' teaching load. While 51 colleges stated that their graduate faculty teach less than if they had a program comprised solely of undergraduate courses, in at least two colleges the graduate faculty actually teach more.

The situation, however, may be worse than this would seem to indicate. The questionnaire was designed with certain internal checks. In answer to the question, "Is there a difference in teaching load between graduate and undergraduate faculty members?" only two colleges reported that the graduate faculty taught more. Yet in answer to the question, "Is graduate instruction considered part of, or over and above, the normal teaching load?" 20 of the institutions listed it as over and above. Three others indicated that it was either or both.

An analysis of the replies indicated that there was frequently a load differential by subject field. For example, in some institutions the professional courses in education, because they were given in the late afternoons and Saturdays, were all considered as being above and beyond the normal teaching load, whereas the graduate courses in the liberal arts and sciences, because they frequently combined undergraduate and graduate students, were given during the day and were incorporated in the regular teaching load. Of course, where the graduate program was limited to the summer, the graduate work was separate from the normal academic year load.

Surprisingly few colleges granted any consideration for the supervision of theses or for participation in arranging or conducting oral examinations. Where a formula was devised for thesis supervision, at best the instructor received one graduate credit for supervising three theses during the semester. That this represents a problem was voiced by the director of one of the best-known colleges in the group: "The guidance of theses and service on thesis committees have never been recognized in faculty loads and therefore constitute a hidden contribution of the faculty that should receive compensation and is a basic source of faculty dissatisfaction with graduate work."

On the visits to the campuses it was evident that there was genuine concern with the problem of the teaching load. Particularly where there was no reduction for graduate courses or where there was differentiation by subject field, the faculty members expressed feelings of discontent, a discontent that is likely to be exacerbated by any expansion of either the undergraduate or graduate program. On some campuses a partial measure of relief is provided by keeping the graduate sections as small as possible and by granting the faculty member the use of one or more graduate students to assist him in some of his clerical details or even in his undergraduate teaching.

44

Many of the colleges provide an extra stipend for teaching graduate courses, a practice which has few or no exceptions when the graduate instruction is considered to be in excess of the normal teaching load. The stipend ranges from $250 to $1,000 for a three-hour course. Oddly enough, some of the colleges admit to no consistent practice. Occasionally one faculty member receives both the stipend and special consideration in scheduling, but his colleague in graduate instruction receives neither. One can observe only that such an institution is likely to demonstrate soon the validity of the observation, "a little college is a dangerous thing."

There seems to be widespread recognition that these related matters of load and compensation represent one of the most ticklish problems with which the graduate administrator has to wrestle. In the large university graduate work is taken pretty much for granted and certain "categorical imperatives" are generally accepted. On the small campus, however, a kind of dichotomy exists. While recognizing the desirability of giving the faculty member every encouragement to devote even greater amounts of time to preparation for graduate instruction, the administrations are faced often with something less than enthusiastic understanding of this principle on the part of the faculty members not directly involved. Thus where no extra consideration is given, the graduate instructor may feel some discontent over his additional and unrecognized responsibilities; on the other hand, where there is extra compensation or reduced teaching, the other faculty members feel discriminated against.

The facts of the situation are that 84 of the 143 colleges provide no difference in compensation for graduate instruction. Only 28 of them recognize the graduate teacher by granting him higher compensation. There is, however, another way to look at this. For, as was emphasized by a number of the respondents, the faculty members concerned with graduate work are the more seasoned and experienced members of the staff and thereby are already at a higher level of compensation than their younger colleagues. Or, as one graduate director observed, while theoretically there is no difference in compensation at his institution, actually it has been necessary to pay more to attract men qualified to conduct graduate work. The ultimate result, of course, may be a relative rise in the total faculty pay scale, to the benefit of all faculty members—undergraduate as well as graduate.

Research. An important factor in the quality of teaching on the graduate level would appear to be the provision made by the college to encourage faculty research. Certainly if one of the principal functions of graduate study is to train a student in the techniques of original investigation, then faculty members themselves should be persons with considerable experience and interest in research. Thus everything possible should be done by the administration to encourage faculty members' activities in this area.

But again, one wonders if the graduate study in the liberal arts college is not in a somewhat different frame of reference. As will be noted later in this study, many of the schools require no thesis for the master's degree. (The larger universities have already pointed the way in this lessening of requirements.) Further, a high percentage of the students in this group of institutions are interested largely in upgrading themselves in their profession of elementary or secondary school teaching. Regardless of the need for soundly conceived and executed research in these areas, there is simply not the interest on the part of the average school teacher, whose daily concerns are quite removed from the abstractions of investigation. Moreover, to return to the college campus, there has not been in the independent, liberal arts college nearly the same tradition of "publish or perish" which characterizes the larger, more established graduate universities.

Therefore it is no surprise that 99 of the 143 colleges, when asked what they did to encourage the graduate faculty members to engage in research, either replied that they did nothing or evaded the issue by stating that they did nothing beyond what was done for all faculty members. The relatively few that answered this question in a more positive manner indicated that they provided the graduate faculty with a reduced teaching load for this purpose (15 colleges), that they made special provisions for leaves of absence (three colleges), that they provided clerical facilities to assist the graduate faculty in research projects (four colleges), or that they provided research grants out of their own resources or assisted the faculty member in obtaining research grants from outside sources (five colleges). One from this last group stressed the intimate association between graduate teaching and research:

> The development of the graduate program was considered one means of encouraging faculty research. The University Research Com-

mittee has since 1946 been increasingly successful in locating financial support for small research projects from foundations. Moreover, it recently reinstituted a program of a one semester sabbatical to encourage faculty research.

Similarly, another of the colleges indicated that "the selection to teach a graduate course is looked upon as an opportunity and incentive to research." "This is especially true," the respondent continued, "in view of the fact that there are relatively few members of the faculty doing graduate teaching."

A few colleges have worked out financial incentives to encourage faculty research. At one, for example, class-hour credit is given on the basis of one credit for approximately four hours of research activity. Another provides "compensation for college-sponsored research up to ten per cent of the salary of faculty beyond the normal teaching load." And a few others indicated that they have available small grants for publication or for research conducted during the summer or for the purchase of books and materials essential to research projects. It was not clear, however, whether these perquisites were limited to the graduate faculty or, as is more likely, whether they were available equally to the total faculty.

It was interesting to the directors of this study to notice that, while a number of the faculty members stressed the advantage of having graduate assistants helping them with personal research activities, this was mentioned in practically none of the questionnaires returned by the officers responsible for the graduate program.

An evaluation of the information received from all sources suggests overwhelmingly that, despite some notable exceptions, faculty research does not seem to be of paramount importance in graduate programs in the independently structured colleges. As one respondent expressed it, "We hold the view that staff members with doctor's degrees who do a good job in directing the research and field study of graduate students have very limited time for individual research."

The Faculty Member and Graduate Teaching. In order to obtain a clearer picture of the attitudes of the graduate faculty toward their teaching duties, questionnaires were distributed to a sampling of 100 faculty members.[2] Seventy per cent of the questionnaires were returned.

2.   See Appendix II, Questionnaire "C."

Among the questions included were two designed to obtain some view of the instructor's personal involvement. He was asked what personal benefits he felt he derived from, and what personal disadvantages he experienced in, participating in the graduate program. Since it is a characteristic of our profession to be articulate, many of the replies were both full and frank. It seems appropriate, therefore, that this chapter should close with a sampling of the responses showing the full range of opinion. With but few exceptions the quotations selected expressed the views of at least three respondents. (We would note, in passing, that the replies are significant also in the implied attitudes toward the undergraduate programs.)

**What personal benefits do you feel derive from
your participation in the graduate program?**

An increase in stimulation to do one's very best in teaching, which includes keeping abreast of all the latest developments in one's field.

The opportunity to get together some new material and teach it without having to figure whether it fits into the undergraduate curriculum.

The opportunity for more thorough preparation for courses, since the course load for teachers in the graduate division is reduced beyond what it is in the undergraduate.

A graduate program necessitates the use of basic tools of thought and research. In undergraduate work, although one may use these tools, he can get by without their constant use. But in graduate school one has no choice. Hence the academic demands of graduate instruction insure a steady and constant intellectual growth.

The opportunity for greater reflection upon the teaching process itself, probably to the improvement of my teaching on all levels and certainly to the better understanding of school policy.

Increased opportunity for discussion centering around real and pressing problems, discussion which is unfortunately lacking (mainly by reason of circumstances) among the faculty.

Increase in editing skill and probably writing facility.

Preparation for graduate courses, requiring almost double my un-dergraduate course preparation time, has brought a higher level of instruction to my undergraduate courses.

Opportunity for directing seminars in special areas of scholarship.

Last summer for the first time in four years I had an opportunity to teach a graduate course in mediaeval drama; in this April issue of *Speculum* I have a slight article published. I certainly would not have written the article had I not taught the graduate course.

An ever-growing interest in research.

Supervising theses not in one's own area of research widens the scope of one's active interests in a way mere teaching does not.

It is convenient to have a ready supply of slightly better-trained as-sistants in my own research.

I admit that I feel a certain sense of pride in teaching graduate classes; it's a bit flattering to be taken out of the mass of "under-graduate class givers."

Pride in the type and quality of work which students can be chal-lenged and frightened into doing.

I am in the academic business to better myself, rather than to be a "dedicated teacher," and consequently I would not have come here had there not been the graduate program. The only reason I did not stay where I was before—at an Ivy League university—is that the department here is better.

In such small groups it is possible to "educate" in the truest sense of the word—to pose problems that challenge individual solution, to open whole fields of interest to the inquiring student.

The advantage to my morale of being with some young people for whom academic study is of foremost importance.

The graduate students' sense of values, reflected in their objectives and motivation, is encouraging and rewarding to the teacher in the graduate program.

The challenge, especially in technical subjects, of teaching persons many of whom are already experts in applied disciplines.

A chance to form associations with students at a mature level, which are likely to continue into professional life.

It makes me see the need of cooperating with other staff members, both in my college and in other colleges.

Meeting with others engaged in graduate instruction.

The summer graduate program brings in professors from other parts of the country with new ideas and points of view.

A little less teaching load (in hours of class time).

Extra pay.

A way to make a little extra money in a manner less calculated than most to interfere with my studies.

To see students expand their intellectual powers, to modify opinions as the result of research, to approach the ultimate truth on a given topic—these constitute our real pay.

What personal disadvantages, if any?

(Roughly one-third of the respondents found no personal disadvantages; an equal number complained of the inordinate demands upon their personal time and energies.)

The graduate department in a small liberal arts college is a drain on the faculty and finances of the school as a whole.

The graduate work usually falls most heavily on a very few people, whose load becomes very heavy indeed, as a result.

So far the graduate program has caused me a good deal more work than my personal benefits from it.

We are not allowed any credit on our teaching schedule for directing a thesis, a job which involves a great deal of time at the best and at the worst can involve seeing the writer of the thesis through panic, nervous collapse, financial crisis, and collision with other members of the thesis committee.

Requires more teaching and administrative time, for which no reduction of responsibility in other areas is made.

For the chairman of a department the time spent in recruiting graduate students is quite an item.

Difficulties growing out of the fact that my graduate courses are given only in the summer, on an accelerated basis.

Teaching off-hours, late afternoons, evenings, and Saturday mornings to accommodate the part-time student, who must pursue his graduate program while holding a full-time position, could be considered a personal disadvantage.

Since ours is a summer program, I am on a bit of a treadmill and, perhaps, I do not replenish my teaching strength for the undergraduate year as much as I would by a summer wholly given over to study, reflection, and rest. I do not "lie fallow" enough.

Work load—in terms of hours spent in reading and editing student theses and projects—takes more time than I want to spare from my family and personal activities.

Doubling in brass in a small college usually leads to spreading one's teaching schedule over a rather large area of the week, thus leaving little time for much careful reading or leisurely meditation. Even if one wished to do so, there is almost no adequate opportunity to continue serious study on one's own, or to make any but the rarest contribution to one's special field of knowledge.

With so few graduate students the faculty has to spend an excessive amount of time training assistants every year.

The graduate student may deserve more than we can give him, and I am left with a feeling of frustration.

Since I have so few students on the graduate level, I take the cases where students cannot perform on the highest level very strongly. With so few students their weaknesses become apparent and I find myself getting upset about them. . . . Also, since there are so few and since I realize that some must graduate, I catch myself growing lax in applying strict standards all of the time to all students.

Sometimes I get annoyed at the attitudes of some students who just go through the motions of working for an advanced degree.

Although the master's candidates, through their thesis work, rapidly become "junior colleagues," the less gifted contribute little to my own research or to the advancement of the undergraduates.

I miss the significant intellectual and social opportunities on a great university campus.

I see no drawbacks for the young assistant professor. The limitations that do exist are for the men at the professor level. Hence, I aspire to be out of here in ten years, unless, perhaps, the college grows appreciably and the general academic climate improves.

Lack of sufficient faculty for mutual stimulation.

The need to guard constantly against becoming entirely removed from the problems of education at the lower levels.

I have to convince some people that a "small institution" is indeed a good school and that mere size does not spell success.

CHAPTER V

The Student

The ingredients for a successful graduate program are, of course, an adequate faculty, suitable facilities, and a student body qualified to profit from advanced study. Whether or not the students in the colleges under consideration are adequate in quality, there is little doubt that they represent a quantitative group of significant proportions.

Although the independent liberal arts colleges offering graduate study comprise about one-fourth of the total institutions in the United States concerned with this level of instruction, in terms of graduate students served these colleges accommodate only about one-tenth of the national graduate school enrollment.[1] However, it is apparent in the enrollment figures evolved from the questionnaires—and it is important to emphasize that *these figures are to be taken as indicative rather than definitive*—the number of students pursuing master's degrees in the private liberal arts colleges is increasing rapidly. In 1950, for example, there were 7,510 graduate students in the 143 colleges surveyed; by 1955 they had increased to 11,805; and by 1960, to an estimated 25,240. The predictions of those in charge of the programs are that this increase will even accelerate in the years to come. It may indeed accelerate substantially if any significant proportion of the

1. Wayne E. Tolliver, *Summary Report on Survey of Students Enrolled for Advanced Degrees: Fall 1960* (Washington: United States Government Printing Office, 1960), p. 3.

colleges now considering the introduction of graduate study should carry through with their plans. Thus it is not unreasonable to predict that the independent colleges may have in attendance as many as 85,000 graduate students within another five years.

Looking at the increase in terms of degrees, in 1950 the 143 colleges granted master's degrees to some 1,390 students; in 1955, to 1,944 students; and in 1960, to 3,140. The relatively low number of degrees awarded in comparison with the total graduate student body is significant, but it is not substantially out of line with the national average.[2] (Nevertheless, one can infer from these figures that the proportion of degrees to students will fall at a substantial rate!)

Although there is no adequate basis for comparison, it would seem a safe conjecture that the percentage of resident to non-resident students in the small independent colleges is lower than that in the graduate programs in the larger universities. Out of the total enrollment indicated for 1960, and excluding summer students, there are only an estimated 3,127 resident graduate students in the 143 colleges. Clearly, then, one of the patterns in this type of program is the commuting character of the student body. Moreover, a substantial majority of the students is engaged in part-time rather than full-time study. It was difficult to derive an accurate figure, however, because of the wide variation among the institutions surveyed in their interpretation of the term "part-time."

Several other characteristics of the group are worth noting. The first is the large number of graduate students in the small colleges who are engaged in summer study only—a total of 12,461. The second is the large number of women enrolled—14,350, a total which exceeds the male enrollment by nearly 5,000. And, finally, among this list of characteristics derived from numerical observation is the large number of graduate students who are engaged in, or preparing for, teaching on the elementary and secondary levels. According to the questionnaires this group comprised about 14,000 out of the total of 25,240 registrants.

As was indicated in a previous chapter, the graduate students in the earlier programs were drawn largely from the undergraduate body

2. Nationally there is one graduate to five enrollees; in the small colleges the figure is one to eight. The many variables in these statistics, however, make exact comparison hazardous.

of the same institution. There may have been some sentiment in this, but the suggestion is that the reasons were perhaps a little more materialistic. Often the better students with limited financial resources were asked to remain for graduate study so that they might provide inexpensive assistance in the undergraduate programs. A number of institutions in the survey were quite candid in indicating that this was the reason why their graduate program was originally instituted. That it is still a reason must be recognized, but its statistical importance has waned considerably. An analysis of the questionnaires indicates that less than five per cent (1,214) of the graduate students in attendance during the survey year were in institutions where they completed their undergraduate training. A number of the colleges had none of their own graduates in their advanced program—as a matter of deliberate policy.

Although nationally the amount of financial assistance for graduate students is increasing rapidly, the opportunities for such assistance in the smaller colleges are not extensive, presumably because of the limited resources of the institution as a whole. Where fellowships are available, the median for the colleges surveyed is $1,500 per annum, exclusive of tuition. In some instances books are provided the scholarship student, as well as free tuition for the wives of married students. The largest number of fellowships and assistantships seems to be in the colleges in the Northeastern part of the United States, with the Middle Atlantic states coming second. In general, though, the opportunities for the graduate student to find means of support through the institution are minimal.

An interesting sidelight on this issue is presented by the chairman of the graduate committee of one of the Eastern institutions, who indicates that the number of part-time graduate assistantships has actually decreased in his institution in recent years because of the fact that research grants have enabled the faculty to engage skilled aides on a full-time basis. From other sources come indications that, because relatively few of the graduate students are giving full time to their study, it has been difficult to find qualified assistants to fill existing vacancies. The survey disclosed, nevertheless, that 51 colleges employed graduate students in a teaching capacity in the undergraduate program, some of them being used quite extensively, as is indicated in Table 10.

TABLE 10

Graduate Students in Undergraduate Teaching

Number of Graduate Students Teaching	Number of Colleges
1	23
2	9
3	4
4	6
5	4
7	3
11	1
15	1

A variety of other services is also performed by graduate students, some requiring the greater maturity and experience which the graduate student is presumed to have. In instances where the tasks could be equally well performed by an undergraduate, there arises the problem, of course, of open competition between the two levels. The range of these services is depicted in Table 11.

TABLE 11

Non-Teaching Services by Graduate Students

	Number of Colleges
Graduate Assistants	60
Personnel Program Aides	11
Dormitory Counselors	11
Library Work	9
Assistants in Athletics	7
Assistants in Language Laboratory	2
Art Gallery and Studio Assistants	2
Assistants to Administrators	2
Work in Campus Industries	1
Public Relations Assistant	1
Accompanist for Music Groups	1
Supervisor of Audio-Visual Aids Center	1
Janitorial Worker	1
Housemother for Off-Campus Residence	1
Clinical Instructor in Speech Clinic	1
Manager of Schedule at College Theater	1
Section Coach in Lower-Division Classes	1

It is significant that 74 colleges have no graduate students performing services within the institution for compensation. The question naturally arises, therefore, as to how the graduate students in small colleges finance their study.[3] If the sample surveyed by the supplementary questionnaire is at all indicative, then there is a substantially different pattern for full-time as against part-time students. Of the former—a relatively small group—approximately forty per cent are receiving some form of financial assistance through the institution. Another twenty-five per cent have found assistance from federal or church agencies, either in the form of loans or outright grants. The remainder are supported by parents, husband, or from their own accumulated resources. One respondent candidly admitted that his graduate study was made possible by the generosity of his working wife.

On the other hand, the part-time students are almost wholly self-supporting, in a majority of cases financing their education out of current income, with perhaps some supplementary help from the institution or from their employer. As for this last, only three students from the sample indicated that their tuition was paid by their employers, another three stating that they received denominational scholarships. Only one held a scholarship from the college itself. From other evidence it appears that where financial assistance is available through college resources, it is almost exclusively reserved for full-time students.

As for the current vocational activities of the part-time students, it was surprising to note from the responses provided by the colleges themselves that many of the M.A. candidates were already engaged in college teaching. Two of the institutions, in fact, stated that all of their graduate students were teaching in college. Another nine estimated that from one-fourth to one-half were so engaged, with another 49 colleges surmising that at least some of their students were now employed in college teaching.

The vocational information, however, is inconclusive, since 80 colleges in the survey seemed to have very little information about

3. See also James A. Davis *et al., Stipends and Spouses: The Finances of American Arts and Science Graduate Students* (Chicago: University of Chicago Press, 1962). This is an interesting report of a study carried out under the auspices of the National Opinion Research Center.

the current activities of their part-time graduate students. In the questionnaires returned by the students themselves, 22 of the 38 part-time students were engaged in secondary school teaching, a figure which can probably safely be projected to the total group. Another five were in active religious service, and the remainder were engaged in a variety of vocational areas, including business, engineering, college administration, and the like. Since only one admitted to being a housewife, this may well be an area where the colleges, with the right kind of promotion, could uncover a significant source of capable graduate students.

The vocational plans of the graduate students, as distinct from their current vocational activities, seem to be largely unknown to those responsible for the conduct of the graduate programs in the small colleges. This is not to say that individual faculty members may not know the plans of individual students, but only that there is little consistent effort to collect this information in any central location. However, from the evidence at hand, the colleges were able to give certain interesting approximations. The largest group, of course, plans to continue or enter the field of teaching, for the most part on the elementary or secondary levels. Since the nature of the graduate programs themselves is a determining factor in this statistic, it presumably explains the relatively small percentage of the participants in these programs who are preparing for positions in industry. Although three colleges reported that all of their graduate students are so directed, another 27 institutions believe that some, but less than one-fourth, of their graduates are preparing for service in industry. One hundred and six either did not know or were of the opinion that none of their graduate students are headed for industrial careers. As for the remainder, the range of vocational choices includes school or college administration, religious service, social service, library work, counseling, nursing, Y.M.C.A. service, research, and so forth.

Of equal interest are the educational plans of the graduate students, and here a rather wide disparity exists between information provided by the colleges and the replies from the student sample. For, as far as the reporting officials know, very few of the graduate students are planning to continue study toward the doctorate. Only two of the colleges report that all of their graduate students expect to go on for this coveted prize; another five believe that more than half will probably continue work for the doctorate; 11 colleges, that one-fourth to one-half will continue; and 46, that some, but less than one-fourth, will continue their study beyond the master's. The majority (79) either do not know or believe that none of their graduate students will aspire to the doctorate.

On the other hand nearly sixty per cent of the random sample of graduate students (63 in all) expect to continue graduate study beyond the master's degree, most hoping to attain the doctorate. Only 25 of the respondents felt certain at this time that they would terminate their formal study at the master's level. To what extent the aspirations of the remainder may represent wishful thinking can only be conjectured; but it is to be hoped that the colleges themselves may be underestimating the situation.

The scope of the survey did not permit any detailed analysis of the course load of the graduate student in the independent college. Nevertheless, one institution provided the useful breakdown shown in Table 12.

TABLE 12

Course Elections in One College

Number of Students	Number of Courses Elected Fall Term, 1960
373	1
41	2
6	3
2	4
1	5

Although one advantage often claimed for graduate study in the liberal arts college is the possibility of small, homogeneous classes, only about one-fourth of the colleges reported that their graduate courses were limited to graduate students. If we look at this from the total number of courses offered rather than the number of institutions, it appears that more than seventy per cent of the graduate courses in the small colleges include undergraduate students as enrollees. Since by and large these undergraduates represent a selected group, the admixture need not necessarily signalize a lowering of standards. As is discussed in Chapter VI, a common practice in mixed courses is for the graduate student to receive credit only if he achieves a grade of B or better. Moreover, he is often required to perform extra work in the form of additional reading or more extensive research papers.

The graduate students have relatively little contact with undergraduates on the campus—a matter of concern to administrators, faculty members, and students alike. The possibility, therefore, that the graduate student might have an impact on the total intellectual life of the campus is rather remote. In most of the institutions, in fact, the graduate student seems to have comparatively little contact even with his fellow graduate students and equally little with faculty members other than those who actually instruct him. A few colleges have taken positive steps to remedy this situation. In one, for example, the drama department accepts the graduate student on the same basis as if he were a faculty member. He is invited to departmental meetings and included in formal and informal social activities. In another institution graduate enrollment is restricted to those who can actually serve on the college counseling staff, which means that they have a close association both with faculty and undergraduates.

If, as Hayward Keniston observes of graduate schools in general, "at most institutions the graduate student is truly 'the forgotten man,' "[4] he would appear to be even more forgotten in the small college. Keniston's solutions for this problem would not be out of the question for many of the colleges in the group under survey: (1) the department should provide a "common room" where members of the staff and graduate students can gather for informal relaxation and talk; (2) each department should provide a work room for its graduate students, a room equipped with a small collection of basic reference works and used for seminar purposes; (3) the college could, for its full-time students, seek some type of living accommodations which would enable them to achieve some proximity. The high percentage of part-time students, of course, would make this third suggestion impracticable for many, if not most, of the institutions in our category.

It is worth noting in passing that a few of the liberal arts colleges are beginning to emphasize the desirability of having foreign students

4. *Graduate Study and Research in the Arts and Sciences at the University of Pennsylvania* (Philadelphia: University of Pennsylvania Press, 1959), p. 45.

in their graduate courses. One, with a relatively small total enrollment, has 20 such students in its graduate program.

In summary, the typical graduate student in the independent college, if one can be synthesized, is a part-time student electing two courses in each regular term and two courses during the summer session. He (or, better yet, she) lives within fifty miles of the campus and attends the college largely because of its geographic availability. On the other hand, he did not attend the college as an undergraduate. His reasons for undertaking advanced work are not so much to prepare himself for still further graduate study as to provide upgrading in his profession. He pays for his own fees and gets little if any outside financial assistance. And while on the whole he is satisfied with the college, he is more closely identified with his undergraduate than with his graduate alma mater. The reason for this latter may well be that his principal objective is not so much to continue his educational development as it is to obtain a better salary, an advancement in position, or to prepare for service in a specialized field.

Student Reaction. The graduate students in the smaller colleges are not unlike the typical alumnus as described some years ago in the study entitled *They Went to College*,[5] in that they seem rather quickly to develop some sense of loyalty for the institution in which they are studying. They are also like the typical American undergraduate, moreover, in that they are fairly articulate in their criticisms. For them, all is certainly not for the best in the best of all possible colleges. The following quotations from the student questionnaire [6] may be of some use, therefore, in characterizing the views of a sampling of graduate students in the independent liberal arts college:

> I have studied through many years, but never felt so much a student as I do at the present time. I read far more; I read critically; I have fine contacts with a dedicated faculty.

> The undergraduate program at this college is very strong. To me it seems that the offering of graduate work by such a college fulfills an external as well as an internal need. . . . In particular, the college

5. Ernest Havemann and Patricia S. West (New York: Harcourt, Brace and Co., 1952).
6. See Appendix II, Questionnaire "D."

preparing public school teachers should offer a graduate program rounding out and intensifying the undergraduate curriculum.

Since I am thirty-six and had no psychology at all in my undergraduate engineering courses, I particularly appreciate . . . admitting me on a sink or swim basis. Larger schools and those with rigid admission requirements would not have accepted me—I know because I inquired.

I enjoy a small graduate school, though confessedly I have never attended a large one. There is good interaction between students and teachers, and students and students.

I particularly appreciate the small graduate enrollments and the close contact with faculty members. Also, I welcome the liberal arts atmosphere.

I feel the college does not have enough straight graduate courses. Many of the courses are merely undergraduate courses where the graduate student must do an extra project in order to receive advanced credit. Further, there are not enough courses available to enable the student to earn the required thirty hours for the M.A. The additional hours are simply "made up" by independent research.

I sense that the faculty has an inferiority complex about the program.

The M.A. thesis should be a three-hour requirement rather than six. It is an exercise in scholarship that is not original work and does not deserve to carry the six-hour weight. I would rather have the benefit of an additional course and a shorter thesis—though not one of less quality.

The faculty of the college is apparently very much opposed to the director of the graduate school, which puts the students in the middle. Also, we are quite well excluded from the activities of the school.

Because there are so few students in our graduate program, I feel a great lack of opportunity for discussion in my field of interest.

I feel that the fact the school does not offer a doctoral program may contribute to greater interest in the master's degree than might otherwise be the case.

The occasional use of visiting instructors who have themselves only master's degrees tends to mar the usefulness of some courses.

The faculty is always ready to give help to any student on any problem, which leaves him with the feeling of being united with the faculty in his academic work.

One thing I would like to see instituted on the master's level is more courses of the independent study type. The undergraduates in this college, through their honors program, can pursue courses at their own rate of speed, with only intermittent guidance from their faculty adviser. I feel such a system is suitable for a graduate program and would strengthen it.

I could hope that the program of the department would be expanded sufficiently to provide at least one course every semester. Otherwise I feel that the offering is quite adequate and well presented.

I would eliminate the Master of Education and the Master of the Art of Teaching entirely and leave only the M.A. and M.S. The watering down of the master's degree to accommodate the ambitious but weak student is a disservice to us all.

There is too much catering to the undergraduate. As a consequence the specific needs of graduate students tend to be overlooked.

Having attended a large state university before entering . . . , I feel from experience that the smaller institution, since it does not have any of the aspects of the "academic grist mill," can make a great contribution to the growth of an individual.

The small independent graduate school is capable of integrating its courses with a philosophy of life. This is real strength since learning must have ultimate purpose and meaning unto itself.

It is my hope that the newness of the graduate program at . . . may turn out to be an asset, since the program can set a precedent rather than follow a tradition.

Because of the relatively small enrollment, it is necessary in many cases to take advanced undergraduate courses at the graduate level. In these cases, the student is expected to demonstrate a graduate comprehension of the material covered. Such criteria are often difficult to employ as a true measure of graduate achievement.

More exclusively graduate level courses could provide greater enrichment for the graduate student.

The graduate student is too often left out, neither fish nor fowl, neither faculty nor undergraduate.

CHAPTER VI

Standards and Curriculum

One of the graduate students included in the survey expressed the wish that the liberal arts colleges would stop imitating the larger universities and, instead, would begin developing distinctive programs of their own. This hope is one which many would share, but the ensuing analysis of the academic standards and curriculums of the smaller graduate programs reveals very little evidence that it is anywhere near realization.

Earl J. McGrath, in *The Graduate School and the Decline of Liberal Education,* concludes that the graduate school exercises a determining influence upon the undergraduate curriculum and that this represents an unhealthy restriction.[1] Whether or not such an influence is determinative in the undergraduate curriculum, there can be no doubt that the doctoral requirements of the large universities are a major force in shaping the standards and curriculums of the master's programs in the private colleges. Even though these colleges expect that a relatively small percentage of their graduates will continue for the Ph.D., their graduate offerings seem to be conceived not so much as ends in themselves, serving their own needs, but as means of ensuring credits acceptable for transfer to the larger graduate schools. In short, there is a disappointing lack of independence in the very group of schools which should be least bound by stultifying traditions.

Since there is, however, some genuinely exciting experimentation, it is the purpose of this chapter to detail the patterns of academic requirements and curricular offerings and then to highlight those programs which stand out from the rest because they edge off the beaten pathways. Many of the colleges, it must be said in all fairness,

1. New York: Teachers College, Columbia University, 1959.

have developed some discrete features; but only where these result in distinctive programs have they been accorded more than passing reference in this chapter.

Standards and Requirements. One of the great debates concerning the master's degree in the United States is whether it represents graduate or merely postbaccalaureate study.[2] Despite the almost universal expression of concern with standards, the impression gained from reviewing the programs in the colleges of this group is that a substantial number of them are essentially extensions of the undergraduate curriculum.[3] This impression is gained not so much from the fact that in 20 of the institutions superior undergraduates may elect graduate courses for graduate credit,[4] thus making a start on their advanced degree, as from the fact that a high percentage of the classes combine both undergraduate and graduate students. Furthermore, the standards of admission in many of the institutions are relatively undiscriminating.

Many of the deans are quite candid in saying that the graduates of their own institutions are urged, if they show marked academic promise, to undertake graduate study in the larger universities. They state further, particularly where their programs are designed pri-

2. Oliver C. Carmichael expressed this issue as follows: "The character of the master's degree in most universities is not such as to build respect for graduate work. . . . In some institutions the first graduate degree is essentially only a fifth year of undergraduate work; in others it is a consolation prize for those who have been unsuccessful in the Ph.D. qualifying examinations; and in still others it is a professional degree for those planning to teach in the public schools. Undergraduates are vaguely aware of these defects in the first graduate degree. The result is that the able student is not attracted to graduate study. There are some institutions that require two years of scholarly work for this degree, but since there are so few of these, they do not affect materially the pictures sketched above." —*Graduate Education: A Critique and a Program* (New York: Harper & Brothers, 1961), p. 146.
3. See Bernard Berelson's discussion on this point in *Graduate Education in the United States* (New York: McGraw-Hill Book Company, 1960), p. 186.
4. John E. Horner of Hanover College, studying the bulletins of 75 institutions, found a total of 14,732 courses open to graduate students, of which sixty-two per cent were also open to undergraduates. "A Dangerous Trend in Graduate Education," *Journal of Higher Education* XXX (March, 1959), pp. 167-68.

marily for elementary and secondary school teachers, that they feel they cannot insist on high admission standards.

A review of the catalogues gives the following picture of the announced requirements for admission (see also Table 13):

Eighty-eight of the colleges made specific note in their catalogues of the fact that the bachelor's degree is required for admission to their graduate programs. Another 11 are willing to accept the degree or its equivalent, the exact meaning of which remains undefined. Fifty-nine of the 88 colleges also state that the bachelor's degree should be from a regionally accredited college. Five colleges, in order to permit their seniors to receive credit for graduate work, require the bachelor's degree less nine hours; four will accept the bachelor's degree less six hours.

TABLE 13

Bachelor's Degree Requirement for Admission to Graduate School

Requirement	Number of Colleges
Bachelor's degree from a regionally accredited college	59
Bachelor's degree	29
Bachelor's degree or its equivalent	11
Bachelor's degree less nine hours	5
Bachelor's degree less six hours	4
No statement concerning bachelor's degree	35
	143

One hundred and one of the 143 colleges made a definite statement that a transcript would be required before the student's admission to graduate study. Whether some form of provisional admission is possible for latecomers is not evident, but it is doubtful that a good candidate would be held up if his credentials were delayed.

Seventy-five colleges require the scores on a qualifying examination, of which 54 specify the Graduate Record Examinations; 14, the Miller's Analogies Test; and one, whose program is limited to teacher education, the National Teachers Examination. Only six colleges provide their own qualifying examination, while 68 have no stated requirement.

Forty-two colleges specify an undergraduate over-all average of eighty per cent or more for admission to their graduate program, with another eight colleges limiting this to a senior-year average of 80 or more. Except for one college which requires a minimum average of C+, none of the others, so far as can be ascertained from the bulletins, specifies a minimum for admission.

Twenty colleges require the student to have completed an undergraduate major in his graduate subject field. Six other colleges will accept either an undergraduate major or a minor in the graduate subject. Of these institutions primarily concerned with teacher training, 18 require undergraduate courses in education before the student is eligible to elect graduate courses in the field. Another 17 call for a certain number of "general education" courses before the student can be admitted to graduate study.

Seventeen colleges provide an opportunity for conditional admission to graduate study, with several giving special consideration to age and experience in lieu of high academic performance on the undergraduate level. Three colleges indicate that the dean might require additional information before the student would be admitted to the graduate program. Only 15 colleges, however, seem to consider the interview as a significant phase of the admissions process.

Education and teaching are emphasized to the extent that 15 colleges demand that the student be certified to teach before he can be accepted in graduate courses. Another 11 call for successful teaching experience and nine for current employment as a teacher.

As for written documentation, four colleges require the applicant to submit an undergraduate paper as evidence of his readiness for graduate study. Twenty are satisfied with letters of recommendation, some from undergraduate instructors, or other statements in evidence of good academic citizenship. Only eight institutions include the submission of health certificates among their admission specifications.

Approximately one-third of the institutions (46) make a distinction between admission to graduate study and admission to candidacy for the degree, with the latter depending usually upon the number of graduate courses successfully completed and the satisfaction of the language requirements, if any. As for the number of credit hours for the degree, a review of the bulletins shows a variation from 24 semester hours required in eight colleges to 36 semester hours in 14 institutions.

The average requirement is 30, with 126 colleges holding to this standard. The distribution of requirements by hours and degrees is presented in Table 14.

TABLE 14

Requirements in Credit Hours for Master's Degree

(Data Based on Examination of Catalogues)

	Semester Hours									Quarter Hours		
	24	26	27	28	30	32	33	34	36	48	60	
Master of Arts	7	0	1	1	45	2	4	0	2	0	0	62
Master of Science	0	0	0	1	18	3	0	0	2	1	1	25
Master of Education	0	1	2	0	31	4	2	1	6	0	1	48
Master of Arts in Teaching	0	0	1	0	12	2	1	2	3	0	0	21
Master of Liberal Studies	0	0	0	0	2	0	0	0	0	0	0	2
Master of Speech (Public Speaking)	1	0	0	0	1	0	0	0	0	0	0	2
Master of Business Administration	0	0	0	0	7	0	0	0	0	0	0	7
Master of Theology	0	0	0	0	1	1	0	0	0	0	0	2
Master of Music	0	0	0	0	8	2	0	0	0	0	0	10
Master of Fine Arts	0	0	1	0	0	1	0	0	1	0	0	3
Master of Physical Education	0	0	0	0	1	1	0	0	0	0	0	2
Total	8	1	5	2	126	16	7	3	14	1	2	184

Since the amount of time required for the completion of graduate degrees has long been a matter of concern, it is interesting to note that only 82 of the 143 colleges have placed any time limit upon their master's candidates. An important factor, of course, in such a requirement is the ability of the college to offer a wide enough range of courses with sufficient frequency to enable the students to meet the requirements in a specified amount of time. As can be seen from Table 15, the colleges which do place a time limit on their candidates have made the limits fairly generous—a reflection of the high percentage of part-time students who must be accommodated in their programs.

TABLE 15

Time Limit within Which Graduation for
the Master's Degree Must Be Achieved

(Data Based on Examination of Catalogues)

Years	Number of Colleges
3	1
4	3
5	23
6	38
7	12
8	3
No statement	61
9 Summer sessions	2
	143

It is interesting, in view of these limits, to note the estimated length of time actually required by the candidates to complete their degrees. Based on the supplementary questionnaires returned by 110 colleges, the distribution is shown in Table 16.

TABLE 16

Estimated Average Length of Time Required
To Complete the Master's Degree

(Data Based on Questionnaire "E")

Average Years Required	Number of Colleges
1	16
2	39
3	36
4	8
5	6
6	2
Indefinite	3
	110

Many of the master's programs in the larger institutions, particularly in programs for elementary and secondary school teachers, have either dropped the thesis requirement entirely or have provided attractive alternatives. It is encouraging, therefore, to be able to report that a majority of the colleges in the group included in this study (76 out of 143) still consider the thesis an integral part of their master's program. From three to six hours of credit are allowed for the thesis. In some of the colleges where an alternative is admissible, the student may develop a project for three hours of credit or substitute six hours of course work for the thesis requirement, a rather common alternative in the larger universities.

The fact that 49 colleges, as far as can be ascertained from their bulletins, have no thesis requirement at all is, of course, discouraging to anyone who feels that the discipline involved in preparing a master's thesis is an essential ingredient in a sound graduate program. As the dean of one graduate school expressed the matter, however, "Why should the student pay to write a thesis in our master's program when he can go to the state university, only a few miles farther away, and get a master's degree for practically nothing without the great trouble of any writing or research?"

Although many graduate schools offering the doctorate have some publication requirement, a review of bulletins from the colleges in this survey does not reveal any such requirement for the master's thesis. Some theses, of course, might well deserve publication in full; but the rising cost of book production, which has already had a sharp impact upon policies governing the printing of doctoral dissertations, would undoubtedly make any such requirement for the master's thesis unrealistic.

One of the major concerns of doctoral study in recent years has been the place of foreign languages in this academic brew. Although traditionally the minimum of two languages was considered indispensable for the doctorate, many graduate schools are now accepting reductions in this recipe, usually by the substitution of another research "tool" for one of the foreign languages.[5] Dr. Hayward Keniston, certainly not a man to accept reductions in standards casually, summed up his views on the place of foreign language in doctoral study as follows:

5.   See F. W. Ness (ed.), *A Guide to Graduate Study* (Washington: American Council on Education, 1960), pp. 24-25.

There is no reason why a group of departments which feel the need of a particular tool or tools in their training of students should impose their requirements on all departments. The most sensible solution is to place on each department the responsibility for deciding what are the tools essential for the work in its field.[6]

In view of this wavering attitude toward foreign languages for the doctorate, it is not surprising to discover that only 40 of the 143 small independent colleges require even one foreign language for the master's degree, most of them specifying it as an admission requirement. And of these, several are content to recognize successful completion of intermediate language study in the undergraduate program as sufficient indication of competence rather than provide their own instrument for evaluation.

As nearly as can be determined from the bulletins, a majority of the colleges have adopted for their graduate and undergraduate programs a common grading system. Thus 82 of the colleges use the letter grades A to F, generally computing averages by means of the quality-point system. A few others use the simple formula of Satisfactory or Unsatisfactory, or the slightly more discriminating one of adding Honors or Distinction to the list of possibilities.

More important than the grading system as such is the standard of performance required for the degree. Here again the majority of institutions follow the simple procedure of requiring a minimum average. For example, 78 of the colleges specify an over-all B average in all graduate courses. In a few, this was further modified by indicating that either none or no more than six hours of C work would be credited toward the degree. There was no indication, however, of the minimum average, if any, required for the student to remain in good standing. It well may be that the observations made by Marcia Edwards in 1944 still apply. In her *Studies in American Graduate Education* she concluded that there are relatively few failures in course on the part of graduate students.[7] On the other hand, it is not uncommon for the low producer to be advised to withdraw rather than to have a required dismissal appear on his record.

6. *Graduate Study and Research in the Arts and Sciences at the University of Pennsylvania* (Philadelphia: University of Pennsylvania Press, 1959), p. 42.
7. New York: Carnegie Foundation for the Advancement of Teaching, 1944; pp. 6-8.

An allied problem is the matter of transfer credits. The large majority of the colleges in the survey are willing to accept some transfer credit, as is indicated in Table 17.

TABLE 17

Number of Transfer Credits Acceptable for Credit

(Data Based on Examination of Catalogues)

Semester Hours	Number of Colleges
6	75
8	5
9	5
10	3
12	2
3	1
4	2
Quarter Hours	
10	1
15	1

The bulletins do not show any grade limitations on acceptable transfer credits, but the assumption is that credit cannot be transferred for courses in which the student's grade is below the average required for the degree in the host college. (It is interesting to note that a few of the institutions specify certain colleges from which they will accept transfer credit. The explanation given is that this represents a form of cooperation between colleges rather than a system of exclusion.)

Curriculum. The academic courses offered for graduate study vary considerably from college to college, ranging from no formal courses in two institutions to more than 500 possible courses in two other colleges. These courses fall into three categories: the graduate-level courses limited to graduate students only; the upper-division courses elected jointly by undergraduate and graduate students, frequently with stated levels of achievement for the graduate student; and the lower-division undergraduate courses open to graduate students with special permission and for a specific purpose. Of these, the first two categories lend themselves to statistical treatment and thus are significant for the purposes of this study.

The median number of graduate-level courses offered in the 143 colleges is 40, and the median number of upper-level undergraduate courses open to graduate students is 120. As for the former, Table 18 indicates their frequency distribution in the colleges surveyed.

TABLE 18

Number of Courses Restricted to
Graduate Students

(Data Based on Examination of Catalogues)

Number of Courses	Number of Colleges
0	25
1-25	31
26-50	34
51-75	19
76-100	15
101-125	8
126-150	7
151-175	—
176-200	2
201-225	2
	143

TABLE 19

Number of Undergraduate Courses
Offered for Graduate Credit

(Data Based on Examination of Catalogues)

Number of Courses	Number of Colleges
0	2
1-50	35
51-100	26
101-150	23
151-200	15
201-250	6
251-300	15
301-350	9
351-400	4
401-450	5
451-500	1
501-550	2
	143

The undergraduate elections were in the main limited to upper-division courses. A study of the bulletins, however, suggests the possible exception of lower-level courses in liberal studies, particularly for teachers whose undergraduate preparation was deficient in such integrated work. Table 19 gives some indication of the range of undergraduate courses available for graduate credit.

Another way of defining the curricular patterns of the colleges in this study is to look at their course offerings by subject field. As Tables 20 and 21 show, the 143 colleges provide graduate credit in 42 areas. However, the master's degree is not necessarily awarded in each of these areas, but the graduate student may elect courses in these subjects, applying the credits earned toward his degree.

TABLE 20

The Subject Matter Fields—Courses Restricted to Graduate Students

(Data Based on Examination of Catalogues)

	Average Number of Courses	Number of Colleges Offering Graduate Courses in Subject
Agriculture	18	4
Art	5	14
Astronomy	0	0
Bible	18	2
Biology	10	49
Business Administration	12	15
Chemistry	8	33
Classics	7	9
Comparative Literature	5	1
Dance	5	1
Drama	0	0
Economics	9	21
Education	22	87
English	11	48
Fine Arts	0	0
French	7	16
Geography	5	1
Geology	5	4
German	5	7
Greek	5	1
History	13	42
Home Economics	5	3

TABLE 20—*continued*

	Average Number of Courses	Number of Colleges Offering Graduate Courses in Subject
Human Relations	0	0
Italian	5	4
Journalism	18	1
Library Science	20	4
Mathematics	8	30
Music	16	19
Norwegian	0	0
Nursing Education	0	0
Philosophy	7	16
Physical Education	7	11
Physics	7	26
Political Science	6	21
Psychology	8	34
Reading	0	0
Religion	14	27
Russian	5	1
Sociology	7	29
Spanish	6	14
Speech	6	15
Visual Arts	0	0

TABLE 21

The Subject Matter Fields—Total Courses Open to Graduate Students

(Data Based on Examination of Catalogues)

	Average Number of Courses	Number of Colleges Offering Courses in Subject
Agriculture	19	4
Art	12	51
Astronomy	5	2
Bible	10	7
Biology	11	78
Business Administration	16	44
Chemistry	10	77
Classics	9	40
Comparative Literature	7	7
Dance	11	4
Drama	8	9
Economics	12	66

TABLE 21—*continued*

	Average Number of Courses	Number of Colleges Offering Courses in Subject
Education	33	120
English	18	94
Fine Arts	5	2
French	7	65
Geography	6	13
Geology	7	26
German	6	50
Greek	5	2
History	17	92
Home Economics	9	21
Human Relations	18	1
Italian	5	8
Journalism	7	14
Library Science	15	8
Mathematics	10	76
Music	20	68
Norwegian	5	1
Nursing Education	10	5
Philosophy	10	66
Physical Education	10	43
Physics	9	67
Political Science	11	71
Psychology	11	78
Reading	5	1
Religion	13	73
Russian	5	14
Sociology	16	75
Spanish	4	59
Speech	11	48
Visual Arts	12	2

Although there are 42 subject matter fields represented, the majority of the offerings in each college in each field were in the category of ten or less courses and many of the courses were not offered annually. Therefore, the tables, because of the flexible character of the various graduate programs, provide only a panoramic view rather than an exact picture. For example, the fact that the upper-division courses were listed as available to graduate students does not mean that graduate students were actually in attendance.

Scheduling. An important consideration in curricular planning is the extent to which specialization is required; or, to express this in another way, the freedom given to the individual to make course elections. A combination of major field requirements and free elections is the usual pattern observed by the 110 colleges that completed the supplementary questionnaire ("E").

Of these colleges, only 31 restricted the student rigidly to the area of his specialization. Seventy-nine required or permitted the graduate student to elect courses in fields other than his area of specialization. Of the 79, 22 specifically required this diversification and 57 made it optional. Table 22 shows the proportion of elections required or permitted.

TABLE 22

Percentage of Total Credits toward Graduation
Which May Be Earned outside the Major Field

(Data Based on Questionnaire "E")

Percentage of Electives	Number of Colleges
0	31
16	22
33	38
50	17
66	2
84	0
100	0
	110

In the questionnaires and in visitation it was evident that the deans placed great emphasis on the advisory process in the arrangement of student schedules. Nevertheless, 38 of the graduate programs call for a particular sequence of courses, 21 of them specifying a strict sequential pattern and 17 providing sequences of courses but permitting some flexibility. Seventy-two of the colleges allow the graduate student to elect courses as they are available and in the order of his choosing, with about half of the colleges stating that the student receives personal guidance in the arrangement of his program.

A number of the deans emphasized the desirability of developing some sequential pattern, despite the administrative difficulties which this involves in the small program. Only by such insistence, they felt, could there be assurance of a degree of homogeneity in the preparation of the student in certain advanced courses. Thus they indicated that specific prerequisites should be encouraged for most advanced graduate courses, prerequisites which could be satisfied on either the undergraduate or graduate level. In this way, too, the student could be prohibited from repeating for graduate credit a course which he had successfully passed during his baccalaureate preparation. It must be added, however, that there was little consistency in the application of this principle among the colleges surveyed.

The Master of Arts for Teaching. The Master of Arts degree for teachers is of particular interest because of its growing popularity. Many of the graduate programs in the colleges included in the study are, in fact, limited to the preparation of elementary or secondary school

TABLE 23

Number of Colleges That Permit Election of Non-Education Courses for the Master of Arts in Teaching, with Semester Hours of Credit Noted

(Data Based on Questionnaire "E")

NUMBER OF COLLEGES

Semester Hours Permitted	Courses for Graduates and Undergraduates	Courses Restricted to Graduate Students	Courses, Level Unspecified	Total
0				
6	7	5	2	14
9	4	1	4	9
12	7	8	8	23
15	9	6	7	22
18	6	2	4	12
21	0	0	0	0
24	0	0	2	2
27	0	0	1	1
30	0	1	3	4
Offer no Master of Arts for teachers				20
Permit the election of no non-education courses				3
				110

teachers. Only 20 of the 143 colleges have no program for teachers as such.

Since one of the questions in this type of program is the relationship between the professional and the subject matter courses, an effort was made in the supplementary questionnaire ("E") to ascertain the number of "non-education" courses, graduate or undergraduate, which the candidate can elect and apply toward his degree requirements. The results are given in Table 23.

TABLE 24

Estimated Percentage of the Normal Graduate Student's Credit Earned in Lecture or Lecture-Discussion Courses

(Data Based on Questionnaire "E")

Percentage of Credit Earned	Number of Colleges
0-20	7
21-40	19
41-60	29
61-80	42
81-100	13
	110

TABLE 25

Estimated Percentage of the Normal Graduate Student's Credit Earned in Seminars—Exclusive of Thesis Seminars

(Data Based on Questionnaire "E")

Percentage of Credit Earned	Number of Colleges
0-20	80
21-40	25
41-60	3
61-80	1
81-100	1
	110

Methodology. In the 110 colleges which filled out the supplementary questionnaire ("E"), the lecture or lecture-discussion method of teaching is used a greater percentage of time than any other method. In the estimated percentage of the normal graduate student's credits for the degree, 55 of the colleges used the lecture or the lecture-discussion method in excess of sixty per cent of the time. The distribution of the graduate student's total academic experience, as defined by the percentage of his total credit hours, among the several types of courses or credit exercises is presented in Tables 24 through 28.

A Closer Look: Some Distinctive Programs. Browning's Abt Vogler could add one note to a second, then a third, and get not a chord but

TABLE 26

Estimated Percentage of the Normal Graduate
Student's Credit Earned in Thesis Seminars

(Data Based on Questionnaire "E")

Percentage of Credit Earned	Number of Colleges
0-20	107
21-40	2
41-60	—
61-80	—
81-100	1
	110

TABLE 27

Estimated Percentage of the Normal Graduate
Student's Credit Earned by the Thesis

(Data Based on Questionnaire "E")

Percentage of Credit Earned	Number of Colleges
0-20	106
21-40	3
41-60	1
61-80	—
81-100	—
	110

TABLE 28

Estimated Percentage of the Normal Graduate Student's Credit Earned through Independent Study—Exclusive of the Thesis

(Data Based on Questionnaire "E")

Percentage of Credit Earned	Number of Colleges
0-20	107
21-40	2
41-60	—
61-80	—
81-100	1
	110

a star. The previous pages of statistics, when added together, certainly provide no such celestial illumination. They do, however, give something of the form and outline of the requirements, curriculums, and methodology employed by the private liberal arts colleges in their graduate efforts.

What cannot be seen from these bare data, of course, are the individual variations which have given to many of the colleges a distinctive quality, setting them aside not only from the others of the group but from the larger university programs as well. Thus, while many of the other colleges may deserve to be included in the following pages, a selection was made on the basis of either representative or unique features, with the objective both of giving the range of programs and of making available for possible adaptation some of the experimental approaches developed by certain of the colleges.

The description of these programs has been held to a minimum and is limited, insofar as possible, to their distinctive features. Except for the programs at St. John's College and Stetson University, which seem to control the opposite ends of the spectrum, thus providing a fitting beginning and end to this section, the colleges are for the most part presented in alphabetical order.

St. John's College

St. John's College is one of two colleges in the study that offer the master's degree without any arrangement for formal class work. Dean Curtis Wilson describes this program as follows:

81

St. John's College awards the degree of Master of Arts. The requirements for this degree are determined by the general task the College has set for itself. They are directly related to the teaching of the liberal arts. They comprise (a) teaching experiences at St. John's; (b) the submission of a thesis.

Anyone who has completed two years of teaching at St. John's College may petition the Instruction Committee of the College to present himself as a candidate for the St. John's degree of Master of Arts.

If permission is granted, the candidate shall submit a thesis to the faculty and stand an oral examination on it.

Before submitting his thesis, the candidate must have the thesis topic approved by the Instruction Committee. The topic must have some bearing on the understanding and practice of the liberal arts.

You will note that the M.A. degree is granted only to members of our teaching staff. No other graduate degrees are granted. There is a possibility that another kind of M.A. program will be set up in the future, probably along the lines of the M.A.T. programs elsewhere, but our plans for this are not yet definite.[8]

Amherst, Mount Holyoke, and Smith Colleges

These colleges all offer the master's degree on their own campus and, in addition, have combined with the University of Massachusetts in a cooperative Ph.D. program.

Amherst has had for many years the subject-centered master's degree, where the student assists in the laboratory or in the classroom, pursues upper-division course work, and conducts the research required for the degree. He is usually on campus about two years and is expected to complete a thesis.

Mount Holyoke's statement of its master's degree program is typical of many programs of colleges offering the degree in the traditional subject-centered arrangement.

A master's degree at Mount Holyoke can be secured in one academic year. Since almost all of our graduate students are also acting as graduate assistants and are therefore working for a department half time and studying half time, the usual span of time involved is two years. . . . Mount Holyoke is not operating a large graduate school. We have an undergraduate student body of about 1,450 students and about 50 graduate students. These graduate students almost without exception are serving the college in some part-time capacity.

8. Letter of December 6, 1961.

Our program for the Master's degree is, I think, a strong and rigorous one, and the work which students do as graduate assistants in many ways supplements study in a very effective way. Because of the small number of graduate students, graduate programs for the Master's degree are not so highly standardized as they would be in a larger institution. In some departments, at least, they are almost hand-tailored to fit the particular students. The college lays down certain general regulations for the Master's degree, but within this rather flexible framework the departments may work out their own arrangements. The requirements of thesis, language examination and the substantial block of graduate work are effective in producing holders of Master's degrees, many of whom go on to the doctorate or go into college teaching or research.[9]

Smith College (which, incidentally, awards an occasional Ph.D.) offers the usual subject-centered Master of Arts degree and also a program leading to the master's degree in social service.

The three colleges combine with the University of Massachusetts in a cooperative Ph.D. program. In the creation of this program, the committee recommended that each of the four institutions continue to offer the master's degree on an individual basis. This would not preclude cooperative effort along the lines already familiar at the four institutions at the undergraduate level, nor would it preclude the master's candidate at any of the institutions applying for admission to the cooperative Ph.D. program.

Although the Ph.D. degree is awarded by the University of Massachusetts, some of the work leading to the degree can be done in one or more of the cooperating institutions. The fact that it is a cooperative Ph.D. degree is to be indicated on the diploma, the permanent record card, and all transcripts, as well as in the commencement program. "Residence" is defined as the institution where the thesis work is being done.

Graduate faculty membership is open to qualified individuals belonging to any of the four faculties. The procedure in appointment is to have the qualifications of the faculty member assessed by a committee of the Graduate Council, which is composed of representatives of each institution. The Qualifications Committee then recommends to the entire Graduate Council, whose affirmative vote is necessary for admission to the Graduate Faculty. The Graduate Council determines

9. From Questionnaire "E," December 9, 1961.

general policy, approves courses and degree requirements, sets admission policies, appoints thesis committees, and in general administers all aspects of the cooperative Ph.D. program. Faculty members from Amherst, Mount Holyoke, and Smith have membership on the Graduate Council.

Participation in the cooperative Ph.D. program by departments of the four institutions is on a voluntary basis. If a department wishes to join the program, it petitions the Graduate Council. Participation by individual faculty members is on a voluntary basis. A member of one faculty, moreover, may offer a graduate course at another of the four institutions.

Other Cooperative Programs. There are several coordinated master's programs developing on the basis of geographical proximity.[10] Two examples of this type of development would be the beginning phase of cooperation in northeastern Pennsylvania among the University of Scranton, Misericordia, Marywood, and King's Colleges, and in the mutual acceptance of up to 12 transfer credits between Hardin-Simmons University and Abilene Christian College in Abilene, Texas. Similarly, Temple University has developed cooperative ties with several small colleges, including Franklin and Marshall in Lancaster, Pennsylvania. Linfield College has a cooperative arrangement with Oregon State University, which enables their graduate students in physics to take advantage of the National Defense Graduate Fellowships. The first year's instruction, equivalent to the master's, is completed at Linfield, and the second and third year are provided by Oregon State. This makes it possible for the graduate student to plan a three-year sequence leading to a doctor's degree and to become eligible for a National Defense Graduate Fellowship.

Some programs with unique cooperative features are the Mount St. Mary's College (Los Angeles, California) graduate program in music, which includes the opportunity of performing with the Los Angeles Symphony Orchestra; the Nazareth College (Louisville, Kentucky) graduate program, which embraces a seminar in human

10. Robert H. Koenker recently explored graduate-level cooperative programs in education and reported that 55 such programs were in operation. See "What's Happening in Teacher Education," *Journal of Teacher Education* X (December, 1959), pp. 507-12.

relations in cooperation with the National Conference of Christians and Jews; and the San Francisco College for Women (San Francisco, California) graduate program that provides for the M.A. in Spanish by combining study on the San Francisco campus with study at extension centers in Madrid (winter) and Valencia (summer), employing professors from the nearby universities.

A cooperative arrangement that may expand to many colleges in the next few years is the plan whereby the liberal arts college serves industry in the education of its employees. With proper controls it is mutually advantageous to both parties. The college can gain facilities, finance, and instruction, while industry can gain training and research centers, both highly important to its well-being.

Among examples of such relationships, Birmingham-Southern College has combined with the Southern Research Institute to offer graduate programs in chemistry and biology for the employees of industry in the Birmingham area. Financial support for the program is provided by the institute. The college departments concerned are responsible for staffing the courses, but there is strong assistance from the personnel of the institute.

Williams College had a similar arrangement with the Sprague Electric Company in nearby North Adams. Sprague has provided the funds (a direct grant) to assist eight of its professional employees in the continuance of their study in the sciences. The men are released from work every Tuesday morning from eight to nine-thirty to attend classes at the college, and one afternoon a week to serve as assistants in the Williams laboratories. (Incidentally, two of these employee-students resigned their positions in industry to become teachers at Williams.)

Alfred University has two arrangements: a cooperative program with Syracuse University and the University of Buffalo leading to the Ed.D. degree and a cooperative relationship with Corning Glass Works in which the college offers courses in physics and chemistry for company employees. Similarly, Wilkes College has participated actively with its community in helping to assure the establishment of a new R.C.A. plant in the area by agreeing to institute a graduate program in the sciences for the training of new employees.

The deans, while cognizant of the advantage of these coordinated plans with industry, are concerned that the program be under the direct control of the college. They considered some of the influential factors in control to be: that the courses be conducted on the campus; that the college teachers do most, if not all, of the teaching; and that college facilities be supported and augmented.

Antioch College

A special degree, Master of Science Teaching, is being offered by Antioch to secondary school science teachers who are taking part in the National Science Foundation's In-Service and Summer Institute Programs.

Colgate University

Colgate University has achieved a reputation for having a distinctive graduate program which consists of advanced academic courses on the undergraduate level and graduate courses in guidance and administration. During the summer graduate courses are provided in all subjects for teachers. The rationale for the academic year program is given in the following paragraphs in the catalogue.

> Colgate University offers studies leading to the Master of Arts degree for college graduates preparing to teach in public school or college. Most graduate students are enrolled in teacher-education programs. M.A. study is restricted to fields represented in the undergraduate curriculum. Outside the Department of Education, which does offer courses for graduate students only, M.A. candidates generally register for advanced undergraduate courses and seminars or in special studies, with additional assignments prescribed for graduate credit.
>
> Graduate work may be pursued either during the academic year or in the Summer Session, but the M.A. degree is available to women in the Summer Session only. General requirements for the M.A. are the same both in the academic year and in the Summer Session.
>
> Graduates of recognized colleges and universities whose work has been largely of a liberal arts character are eligible to apply.

There are actually four distinct programs offered. One comprises 30 hours of work in an academic field, including a thesis, as the first step toward the Ph.D. and college teaching. Studies are restricted primarily to the following fields: American civilization, English, history, political science and international relations, philosophy and religion, and psychology. Under certain circumstances, programs can be arranged in sociology but are not available in M.A. work devoted strictly to a foreign language and its literature, economics, mathematics, or any of the individual sciences.

One unique feature of this plan is the Preceptorial Program. The graduate student is assigned half-time duties as a freshman adviser, devoting the remainder of his time to graduate study. Preceptors are considered junior members of the faculty, attend faculty meetings (without vote), and are welcome at faculty events, including those held at the faculty club. This program has made possible a fortification of the college guidance and counseling division, and has trained men who have subsequently assumed college administrative positions.

The second program, involving both education and subject matter courses and, generally, a thesis in education, accommodates most of the graduate students. The resultant degree, considered to be terminal for secondary school teachers, places its stress on liberal arts preparation.

Colgate also has a combined undergraduate-graduate program, a concept which is gaining increasing support in some of the more advanced thinking about the master's degree: [11]

> Colgate offers a five-year program leading to the degree of Master of Arts in Teaching. Beginning in the junior undergraduate year, sequences of courses, individual projects and field work are available to prepare men for secondary school teaching in one of these basic fields: English, social studies, sciences, mathematics, foreign languages, physical education—or some combination thereof; also for Guidance and Administration, after preliminary teaching in a subject field. All of these teaching-area programs . . . are devised not merely to meet the professional teacher-certification requirements of New York and nearly all other states, but to provide a liberal education in the teacher's subject field.

> With the exception of the teaching of Physical Education the fifth (graduate) year of this program is available also to approved candidates who have earned Bachelor's degrees in other institutions. All candidates, including Colgate graduates, must apply for admission to the Committee on Graduate Studies, and meet the university standards established for such work. Personal qualifications for teaching are also reviewed at the time of admission to the fifth year. A minimum of nine hours of graduate work must be done in the Department of Education.[12]

11. See Carmichael, *op. cit.*, pp. 162-77.
12. *Colgate University Catalogue 1960-61*, p. 69.

As was indicated, the five-year program for secondary school teachers in physical education is a unit and is available only to students who begin it as Colgate undergraduates. The fifth year is devoted to advanced work for certification to teach physical education and an academic subject in secondary schools, and to meeting other requirements for the degree of Master of Arts. These requirements may be completed either in one year on a full-time basis or over a longer period as a teaching intern.

Colgate is engaged in a fourth program, a cooperative internship for secondary school teachers with some of the larger schools in the Central New York area. The purpose of this program is to strengthen the preparation of teachers and to attract more liberal arts graduates into teaching. It enables selected men graduates of four-year colleges to begin public school teaching while completing their requirements for full certification and the Master of Arts degree. Interns enter the program in the summer with enrollment in a special summer session that includes student teaching. Interns devote half the following academic year to full-time graduate study and teach the other half. Each intern receives a minimum salary of $2,100. While obtaining supervised experience as teachers they complete their academic and professional education during the academic year.

The Summer Session for Teachers at Colgate possesses a unique feature in that planned sequences of graduate seminars are provided in social science, science, mathematics, and English. There are also seminars in guidance, curriculum development, and in administration arranged in four-year sequences. Undergraduates are not eligible. Teachers may work on their own problems in any of these seminars or they may enroll in a special studies course on a tutorial basis. Qualified students may earn the Master of Arts degree in four summer sessions. The major features of this program are: (1) individual instruction; (2) unified sequences; (3) emphasis on improvement and reorganization of curriculum content.

In addition, national and state institutes are being offered in foreign languages, mathematics, science, counseling and guidance, and summer research. In these programs teachers receive free tuition. The national programs also provide stipends.

One final statement from the Colgate catalogue is worth special emphasis here: "Graduate students will be accepted only when it is clear that the University can provide a suitable program to meet the needs of the student." Nevertheless, there were 442 graduate students enrolled at Colgate in all sessions in 1960.

College of the Holy Names *(Oakland, California)*

The purpose of this program is the preparation of college teachers. In the field of English, as an example of the success of this endeavor, all but one of its graduates are either already in college teaching or about to enter, preparing for it by doctoral study, with supporting scholarships or fellowships. A majority of those holding the M.A. in English have gone on for the Ph.D. The graduate dean attributes much of this success to the fact that the graduate division is small and the contact between professors and students is frequent and informal. The teaching assistants are given a great deal of direct supervision both from their professors and from the departmental chairman.

Goucher College

Goucher College has a master's degree curriculum for the preparation of elementary school teachers which is designed to provide intensive preparation for selected men and women graduates of accredited liberal arts colleges for teaching in grades one through six and to add to the number of well-prepared, qualified elementary school teachers. A pre-session of four weeks in September and an academic year of two semesters make it possible for a student to earn the degree of Master of Education. Three courses are taken during the pre-session; six courses during the first semester; and one course (seminar) during the second semester concurrently with a teaching internship in the Baltimore City area at a salary of $2,100.

Hollins College

Hollins College has master's programs in psychology and creative writing. The former is experimental, and the student is expected to engage in intensive research. In the program in creative writing the student is required at the end of the year to produce a volume of short stories or poems, a novel, or an extended critical essay in satisfaction of the thesis requirement.

Incarnate Word College *(San Antonio, Texas)*

A distinctive feature in the graduate program at Incarnate Word College is its course entitled "Pro-Seminar," which provides an introduction to educational research. This seminar, designed to help the student in his orientation to graduate study, is the first course to be studied in the graduate program.

Loyola University *(Los Angeles, California)*

Loyola University offers an unusual Interdisciplinary Seminar in Contemporary Thought in its program for the Master of Arts. Serving as a medium of interdepartmental association among both faculty and graduate students, the seminar is intended to overcome the criticism frequently made of the excessive departmentalization and professionalization of graduate programs in the United States. It is also planned to afford a constructive solution to some of the problems resulting from extreme specialization. The seminar provides for discussion and analysis of contemporary thought as revealed in the following areas: (1) history and political science; (2) natural science; (3) sociology and psychology; (4) economics; (5) philosophy and theology; (6) art, language, literature.

Marywood College *(Scranton, Pennsylvania)*

Marywood College offers a course in comparative education taught by seven professors, five of whom are natives of the countries on which they lecture. Currently the lectures are on primitive, Greek and Roman, Italian and Spanish, French, German, Austrian, Russian, and Indian systems of education. Foreign student panels and films are employed as supplementary features.

Mercer University

One important feature of the Mercer University graduate program is the training of teachers as cooperating teachers to supervise student teachers.

Middlebury College

During the academic year, the Middlebury College Graduate Schools of French in France, German in Germany, Italian in Italy, and Spanish in Spain provide indispensable guidance in the complexities of advanced study at a foreign university, with the opportunity to earn a Middlebury master's degree by a year of supervised foreign study.

Oberlin College

Oberlin College began a program for the Master of Arts in Teaching in June, 1960, with Ford Foundation support for a five-year period. The college assists 20 graduate students in their preparation for secondary school teaching positions in an internship program that can be completed in one academic year and one summer. The student elects 15 credit hours during the first semester, does an internship in an area school and attends a seminar on Saturday mornings in the second semester, and studies educational psychology and has a seminar on methods during the summer. He receives a stipend of $1,500 for his teaching and a supplementary grant of $800.

Ohio Wesleyan University

Ohio Wesleyan University has a unique program in graduate study in English. Five graduate students are admitted with the opportunity to do half-time study in advanced undergraduate courses and with the responsibility to assist in the English department. The students are required to tutor undergraduates who have received two grades of "unsatisfactory" in writing in any course or combination of courses. The undergraduate student is tutored until his writing ability is approved by a committee chaired by an English instructor. The graduate student receives a stipend of $1,600 per year and a tuition grant. He usually takes two years to complete his master's degree, which includes a thesis requirement.

University of Redlands

In addition to its own master's programs, with an emphasis on breadth and consideration of the student as an individual, the University of Redlands is one of seven colleges participating in the Intercollegiate Program of Graduate Studies. All are independent liberal arts institutions with enrollments ranging from 250 to 1,300 students and located within thirty-five miles of a common geographical center in Claremont, California. Through the pooling of facilities they provide an exceptional opportunity to combine the advantages which size gives to a large university with those valuable assets which are generally found in small liberal arts colleges.

The cooperative doctoral program enjoys the assistance of grants from the Fund for the Advancement of Education, from the Ford Foundation, and from the John Randolph Haynes and Dora Haynes Foundation. Fellowships under the National Defense Education Act are also available for students in the program.

St. Mary College *(Xavier, Kansas)*

At St. Mary College a consultant in written English is available to graduate students and the total faculty assumes responsibility for the quality of their written work. A program planning sheet that permits the student to plan his courses over a seven-year period is also an unusual feature.

Sarah Lawrence College

Sarah Lawrence began its program in graduate study because the members of the faculty were of the opinion that there was need "to make of the undergraduate and graduate programs such a combination of significant intellectual and personal experiences that the student will come to recognize in the work of the college teacher that high calling which has always marked the profession of the true scholar and the true teacher." [13] Therefore, with the basic thought that the making of teachers was an important aspect of the undergraduate program, the college believed that the smaller residential colleges for the liberal arts had special opportunities and obligations for developing good graduate students, particularly since in "the smaller institutions, the pressures toward patterning are, or at least should be, less."

The basic purpose and procedures of graduate instruction at Sarah Lawrence College are patterned on the principles which operate in the

13. *A Graduate Program in an Undergraduate College,* ed. Charles Trinkaus (Middletown, Conn.: Wesleyan University Press, 1956), p. xi. Subsequent references to the Sarah Lawrence program are all from this publication.

undergraduate college.[14] As in the college, no formal over-all program is designed. Advanced study is planned in terms of individual student needs and individual student purposes, not in terms of credits and courses.

Sarah Lawrence College received a grant of $50,000 from the Carnegie Corporation to begin the work of its graduate program. The publication in relation to its program, *A Graduate Program in an Undergraduate College*, is a most useful and comprehensive explanation of the master's degree in one small independent liberal arts college and is recommended for study by any college conducting or contemplating the offering of a graduate program.

Swarthmore College

Swarthmore College also incorporates the distinctive features of its undergraduate into its graduate program. The departments offering the

14. "The undergraduate program at Sarah Lawrence was established in 1928, when the College opened, as an experiment in the reform of liberal education. In place of the conventional curriculum of the elective system or of the required sequences of departmental courses, the faculty has built a program in which each student plans an individual curriculum of courses with the help of faculty advisers. In addition to the general curriculum of liberal arts, the creative arts, painting, drawing, sculpture, music, design, theatre, dance, and writing have been installed as regular elements of the curriculum itself. Instruction is conducted by the seminar and discussion method, with regular weekly conferences between the faculty member and his students, and the lecture used only occasionally when it is considered appropriate. Science is taught in the laboratory with student research; theatre is taught on the stage as well as in the classroom; social science through field projects; child psychology in the nursery school; literature, history, philosophy through original sources with only occasional reference to textbooks, anthologies, or surveys. The aim throughout the teaching program is to confront the student directly with the materials and methods of each branch of knowledge and to make them real in his experience. Courses are planned on a full-year basis, and, in a given year, students work in three courses rather than the usual five or six. There are no organized departments, and no majors, although students who wish to work in a given field as one-third of the year's program throughout the whole four years are usually allowed to do so. Field work is a regular part of each section of the curriculum. The examination, grading, and credit system is replaced by a system of reports made twice each year by the faculty members on the basis of the work of the student in class, in independent research projects, and in conference. There are no subject-matter requirements for graduation other than the successful completion of four years of study as approved by a faculty committee which supervises the course of study of each student."

master's, such as astronomy, history, philosophy, and psychology, require either three or four seminars and a thesis for the degree. These seminars are the regular honors seminars provided for the undergraduates in the independent study program. As a result the students who have received the bachelor's degree from Swarthmore are not normally eligible for this work. The departmental chairman determines the admission of the graduate student and informs the Graduate Committee when the student is admitted. As in the undergraduate program, the work of the seminars is judged by external examiners.

Texas Wesleyan College

Texas Wesleyan College has a first course that serves somewhat as a proving ground. All new graduate students are required to attend a foundation seminar in which they are screened as to their leadership, scholastic and teaching abilities, and their ability to use the English language effectively.

Wesleyan University

Among the more distinctive Master of Arts in Teaching programs is the one at Wesleyan University. Dr. Victor L. Butterfield, in describing the objectives of the program, writes as follows:

> Our hope, in the last analysis, can be fulfilled only if our students can capture insights into what it is that can dignify a man and make his life significant both as a person and as a citizen.
>
> Because we hold such a conviction, in the midst of a society that has grasped the importance of "how" but is feeling only tentatively the importance of "what," Wesleyan seeks to solve some of the problems that perplex public education. It is not that we have *the* answers. It is rather that we have resources which may assist some prospective teachers in their search to discover the profounder meaning of their own lives and therefore the lives of those they teach. It is, we hope, a timely and vital if limited service, which may narrow the gap between "methods" and "substance" and bring to students an organic experience in education in which they can learn both what it means to be adults and citizens, and how they can achieve this meaning for themselves.
>
> Wesleyan's Master of Arts in Teaching Programs are attempts to provide such experience. They are designed to give future teachers an opportunity to deepen their own insights through continued study in

the liberal arts or sciences and to give them the necessary elements in the art of teaching. We hope that the programs will prepare a number of men and women each year to put their training and experience to effective use in the public schools. We trust that with deepened understanding and broadened interest they will become better leaders in our common cause.[15]

Wesleyan actually offers two programs leading to the Master of Arts in Teaching. In the two-year program the student has an apprenticeship or salaried internship in teaching, elects a sequential pattern of courses in education, and pursues 21 semester hours of course work in his major or minor teaching fields or in related areas. Another feature of this program is that it leads to the Master of Arts in Teaching and a Diploma of Further Study. The diploma indicates the extent of work accomplished beyond the master's degree during the two years of study in residence.

The one-year program can be completed in one academic year and one summer session. The prospective student is required to have had a strong undergraduate major in the subject he plans to teach and to have taken some previous course work in education. The M.A.T. degree is awarded on the completion of 30 semester hours of credit, including a maximum of 18 and a minimum of 12 hours in the subject the student plans to teach.

There is an opportunity in both the two-year and the one-year programs for flexibility. The student may select upper-level undergraduate courses or graduate seminars, or he may pursue independent study under faculty tutorial assistance. Classroom teaching and certain education courses are required, but students are expected not to repeat work taken as undergraduates. Therefore the number of education courses and the amount of student teaching will vary according to previous experience and need.

In addition to the regular course work the students are strongly urged to take advantage of the opportunity to participate in field work, a distinctive feature of the program. Although no academic credit is given, the candidates devote from eight to 12 hours a

15. *Master of Arts in Teaching* (Middletown, Conn.: Wesleyan University, 1960), pp. 3-4. See also Joseph S. Butterweck, "A Post-Baccalaureate Program in General Education," *Liberal Education* XLVII (December, 1961), pp. 483-91.

week to this activity in at least one of three areas: athletic coaching, extracurricular activities in local high schools, or community activities. The purpose of this experience is to enable the teacher to make a more significant contribution to his school and community.

Williams College

One of the unique experimental programs is the Center for Development Economics at Williams College. Founded in the fall of 1960 under a $423,000 grant from the Ford Foundation to institute a new graduate training program in development economics for students from Asia, Africa, and Latin America, the center represents the first effort by a small college to help, through graduate training, to meet the problems of underdeveloped countries.

The first 20 students who were selected came from 17 foreign countries. Some of the students were junior civil servants employed by development agencies, ministries of finance, or central banks in underdeveloped countries. Others were staff members of business firms and private organizations figuring prominently in the national economic life. All were assured that on return to their country they would be employed in a post which would enable them to put to effective use the training received.

In addition to weekly field trips during the academic year, the students participate in a six-week summer field trip at the end of the academic year to supplement their studies. This trip covers some 5,000 miles through New England, to Chicago and Washington, and includes visits to industrial plants, schools, government facilities, and other relevant institutions.

It should be observed here that several of the small colleges enroll graduate students from foreign countries (Smith had 15 in 1960), but the Williams program is the only one exclusively designed for foreign students.

Stetson University

Stetson University, the description of whose program will bring this chapter to a close, has for the past several years been planning and preparing to offer a five-year program leading to the Master of Philosophy degree and designed to prepare selected scholars for careers in college teaching, particularly for the junior colleges. Recently (September, 1961) the university received a Ford Foundation grant of $223,000 to be used over a five-year period for this purpose. The program will begin at Stetson in the fall of 1962 with the participation of selected college juniors. The Florida State Department of Education has lent support to the program and agreed to approve for certification all recipients of the degree.

In a statement of the plan prepared by a faculty committee under the chairmanship of Dean William Hugh McEniry in September, 1960, the need was described as follows:

> With the enrollments in colleges and universities reaching unprecedented peaks, the need for qualified instructors to staff these institutions constitutes the central challenge for higher education today. This situation is heightened in Florida where ten public junior colleges have been established within the past three years and where ten additional junior colleges are scheduled to commence operations within the next five years. At the present time, these junior colleges are being staffed in part by teachers drawn from secondary schools. This procedure further weakens the structure of public secondary education— an area that can ill afford this loss.[16]

The aim of the program is "to tap a potential source of college teachers that has been largely overlooked." In substantiation of this aim the point is made that many capable students have veered away from teaching because of the seeming lack of an intellectual challenge. Others have found the possibility of obtaining the Ph.D. fraught with too many uncertainties.

Another deterrent is seen in the absence of any specific plan that would enable the qualified student to see his way to the fulfillment of his goal as a college teacher. Thus, while enabling the graduate of the Stetson program to begin teaching at an early stage of his academic progress, the plan also looks deliberately forward to the Ph.D. at a cooperating institution after two years of additional study.

16.   "Proposed Five-Year Master of Philosophy Program Designed to Prepare Selected Scholars for Careers in College Teaching, Particularly for the Junior Colleges," prepared by the Committee on Graduate Study of the Faculty of the College of Liberal Arts, Stetson University, De Land, Florida, September, 1960, p. 1. Subsequent references to the Stetson program are all from this publication.

Because of the many promising, if not unique, aspects of this program, it seems appropriate to present it in some detail, using the description provided by the planning committee.

Admission. Undergraduates who have completed two years of general education may qualify for the college-teacher program leading to the Ph.M. degree in one of three ways:

1. Through the Honors Program. Entering freshmen whose predicted grade averages, based upon their high school records and College Board scores, place them in the upper 15 per cent of their classes will be encouraged to enter the Honors Program. The distinctive feature of this program is its integration of broad areas of our cultural heritage that are taught where serious students are grouped together. The first two years of the curriculum include three semesters of honors seminars in the humanities, two semesters of honors seminars in the social and behavioral sciences, two semesters of Western Civilization, two semesters of mathematics, two semesters of natural science, two semesters of Christianity and Western Thought, four semesters of foreign languages, and electives for a total of sixty-three hours. Upon the recommendation of the Honors Committee, candidates who have demonstrated the competencies requisite to success in college teaching will be admitted to the Master of Philosophy Program without further examination.

2. Through the Regular General Education Program. Stetson students who were not in the Honors Program but who have shown exceptional ability in their first two years of work will be urged to apply for admission to the college-teacher program. These students will have had the same type of academic background as the Honors Program students since both will have completed similar general education courses. In addition to the recommendation of his major professor in his chosen field of specialization, each candidate will be required to pass written examinations to qualify for admission.

3. Through General Education Programs at Other Colleges. It is expected that a substantial number of transfers from other liberal arts colleges as well as graduates of junior colleges will be interested in applying for admission to the college-teacher program. These students whose records justify their consideration for the Ph.M. Program may qualify by passing intensive written and oral examinations.

The Third and Fourth Years. The program for each superior student during his junior and senior years will be carefully planned and supervised by the faculty committee responsible for his particular area of specialization. The emphasis at this stage will be to encourage each student to become a *bona fide* participant in the scholarly endeavors of the academic profession by developing within him the skills, attitudes, and the power of independent judgment which are hallmarks of the educated man.

Such an approach will call for intense concentration in the student's major field of endeavor in order that he not only will know his subject but that he also will see himself and his own speciality in relation to other selves and other areas of inquiry. Under skillful direction, he will read widely and critically. Through tutorials, he will develop the capacity to express himself responsibly and with mature reflection. In the seminars, where he is confronted with challenging ideas in company with other superior students, he will learn to think objectively and with the detachment that is characteristic of sound scholarship. To prepare him for his graduate work, he will submit research papers regularly, culminating in the senior essay in which he will demonstrate the ability to conduct a scholarly investigation in the manner that is expected of candidates aiming for the highest degree in the field. He will select the topic for his senior essay with care, for it will be used in his fifth year as the basis for his Master's thesis.

Thirty-eight semester hours will be required in the field of his specialization. In addition to the course work in his major field, each candidate will be oriented to teaching through professional courses especially designed for college teachers. These courses will deal with the social and philosophical foundations of education, the junior college curriculum, and the psychological foundations of learning. A major concern, even during the early phases of his preparation, is to see that each candidate is given the opportunity to observe and teach in the classroom. In his senior year, each student will be assigned to a professor in the department of his specialization as the research and teaching assistant in one course. The major professor will work closely with the candidate to acquaint him with the many facets and practical concerns of college teaching.

Upon the successful completion of this course of study the candidate will be awarded the Bachelor of Arts degree.

The Fifth Year. Before the student is admitted formally to candidacy for the Master of Philosophy Program, his thesis must have been approved, and his record of progress evaluated by his committee. The committee that screens applicants will be looking for the following traits in each candidate: the ability to write accurately with logical organization, to express himself verbally with effectiveness, to listen with retentiveness and perception, and to read rapidly and critically. Mature students who have a mastery of these practical skills and who have demonstrated through performance that they can benefit from, and make contribution to, a life devoted to intellectual activity will be selected.

The program in the fifth year will have two basic purposes: (1) to give each candidate practical experience in college teaching, and (2) to increase and broaden his knowledge in his subject-matter speciality.

The practical teaching experience of the candidate will continue under the plan that began in his undergraduate program. He may elect one of two methods of completing the internship requirement. Under Plan A, he will observe and teach, for which six semester hours of credit will be awarded, in the Early Admission and Advanced Studies Program, College Skills Program, or regular summer session at Stetson University. His specific assignment will depend upon his special field of interest. Three semester hours will be taken in the Practicum in College Teaching in which the interns and their major professors will meet to discuss the problems confronted in their particular situations and the procedures and techniques that contribute to superior instructional programs.

Under Plan B, the candidate will intern in the fall semester under an expert teacher at one of the five junior colleges within ninety minutes drive from De Land. The arrangement of his field work experience will be such that the candidate will teach in the neighboring junior college three days a week and be on campus the other three days. This will enable him to attend the seminar on the Practicum in College Teaching and to continue his independent study for his thesis.

If the candidate elects Plan B, nine hours in course work will be taken the previous summer. For those who completed their internship during the summer under the alternate plan, twelve hours in course will be taken the fall semester.

The final semester for a candidate under either plan will be devoted to seminars in his major field and in related disciplines. The objectives here will be to consummate his preparation for college teaching by giving him a broader perspective of the relationship of his discipline to other fields, and to realize the particular responsibilities assumed when one becomes a part of a community of scholars.

The successful completion of his course work and his internship, the acceptance of his Master's thesis, and the demonstration in an oral examination of the mastery of his field of specialization as related to his thesis will qualify the candidate for the Master of Philosophy degree.

Stetson has every reason to believe that there will be a sufficient number of capable students available to begin a viable program.

Fifty-two freshmen were invited by the university to participate in its honors program in September, 1960. In addition 25 students have entered the summer program of Early Admission and Advanced Studies sponsored, in part, by the National Science Foundation. All of these are potential long-range candidates for the Ph.M. degree.

The faculty members are enthusiastic in their support of the program and are willing and ready to cooperate providing appropriate adjustments can be made in their teaching loads. As for qualifications, over sixty-five per cent of the faculty of the College of Liberal Arts at Stetson University hold terminal degrees.

The sponsors of the program believe a particular advantage to the university's developing this plan is that the master's degree is the only advanced degree that can be earned at the institution. To quote the committee, "Unlike large state and private universities where the Master's degree is acquired leisurely enroute to the doctorate and where there is a consequent de-emphasis of its importance, the concentration at Stetson is upon its M.A. program. The pride that the Stetson faculty has always taken in its graduate students will be enhanced when it is known that its Master's degree candidates will be qualified to teach on the college level."

The program is graphically summed up in Table 29.

TABLE 29

Summation, Expressed in Semester Hours, of the
Third, Fourth, and Fifth Years of the Ph.M. Program

	Third Year	Fourth Year	Fifth* Year	Total
Major Field	20	18	12	50
Thesis and Research Seminar		3	6	9
Supporting Fields	6	6	9	21
Professional Preparation	6	3	3	12
Teaching Assistant and Internship		3	6	9
	32	33	36	101

* Includes one summer session.

Conclusion. The criticism is made elsewhere in this report that much too little of an experimental nature is being attempted by the small colleges in their graduate programs. This is a valid criticism. Nevertheless, as is revealed in the preceding pages, much is being done by a relatively few institutions which is not only educationally significant but which should provide encouragement to the other colleges to go and do likewise. For the ultimate value of the independent college in the area of graduate study depends largely upon its ability to provide progress of genuine and distinctive worth. As Dean J. Peter Elder of the Graduate School of Harvard has noted, "The Master's degree is, at present, a bit like a streetwalker—all things to all men (and at different prices)." [17] But, as he points out later in the same article: "No one can fail to realize how vitally important are the kind and quality of the men and women who teach the youth in our liberal-arts colleges. Present support for our Ph.D. programs is excellent—and desperately needed—and must continue. But we need another kind of support—this time for a host of Master's programs, especially in our well-qualified colleges." [18]

17. "Reviving the Master's Degree for the Prospective College Teacher," *Journal of Higher Education* XXX (March, 1959), p. 133.
18. *Ibid.*, p. 136.

CHAPTER VII

Finance and Facilities

In Chapter I the conjecture was made that few or none of the colleges in this group engaged in graduate study with the idea of losing money. This is not to say, of course, that they engaged in graduate study with the opposite—the hope of making money. Nevertheless, one of the most difficult phases of this entire survey was concerned with the financing. For relatively few of the respondents seemed to know with certainty whether their programs operated in the black or in the red. Although only 17 colleges stated positively that their programs were not self-supporting, 44 indicated that the undergraduate income helped to support their graduate offerings.[1]

On the subject of financing graduate study there are two widely accepted concepts. The first is that graduate education of high quality is far more expensive than undergraduate education of comparable quality. With this there can be little argument. The second is that graduate programs never carry their own weight financially. With this there is some contradiction in the evidence evolved in this study. The combination of these two concepts, moreover, may be partly responsible for the difficulty encountered in eliciting the desired financial data. For many of the colleges which may actually realize surpluses in the operation of their graduate departments seemed reluctant to make the admission, possibly on the theory that this would reflect upon any estimate of the quality of their programs.

1. See p. 107.

But the foregoing may be a complicated interpretation where a more direct explanation is available.[2] The truth is that a substantial percentage of the colleges do not know the answers to budgetary questions for the simple reason that they do not budget the graduate program separately from the undergraduate (at least 72 out of 143 make no distinction between the two). Even where they are differentiated, it is often merely a separate line item in a departmental budget, which could certainly not reflect the full cost of the graduate program. For example, where is the administrative overhead? Conversely, some of the institutions budget separately for the administration of the program but make no distinctions in the departmental budgets. Others differentiate only to the extent that graduate assistants are given a separate code number and charged to the department utilizing their services.

Undoubtedly size plays a significant role in what might otherwise seem to be an unsophisticated approach to the financing of graduate study. Many of the respondents from the smallest schools indicate that the limited graduate commitment makes separate budgeting almost redundant. On the other hand, some of the schools which do budget separately offer graduate study in the summer only or finance it under special grants or endowments. In such instances discrete accounting is virtually mandatory.

Perhaps the examination of financial practices should be looked at in two stages: the first, those involved in inaugurating graduate study; the second, the financial problem of its continued maintenance.

As for the first, several colleges indicated that the initial year (in some instances two to three years) of their program was subsidized by a grant from the trustees. A few, but very few, were fortunate enough to obtain foundation support at the very outset, thus enabling them to get off to a good start. In each instance where this occurred the college already had an established reputation for educational excellence. Moreover, the program which received the support had features that were both experimental and distinctive. For example, several of the colleges in this group received grants to begin their own special versions of the Master of Arts in Teaching.

2. Because the answers returned in the general questionnaire were so inconclusive on this subject, a supplementary questionnaire on finances and facilities was utilized to support and validate the data evolved from other sources. See Appendix II, Questionnaire "E."

In one college a campaign for funds was successfully undertaken with the expressed purpose of underwriting the new graduate program; and in several, where advanced study was initiated as a form of service for local industry, support was received in the form of tuition payments (in one instance, triple the usual fee), overhead, and equipment from the industries being served. At one college this latter also included the services of several dollar-a-year faculty members from the cooperating companies. This, of course, suggests still another form of subsidy—the contributed services of faculty who are clerical members of a supporting church or religious order. In three colleges these services provided an estimated sixty per cent of the cost of operating the graduate courses.

Once under way, the graduate programs carry themselves by a variety of means. The fortunate few are totally subsidized, as has been said, by outside grants (such as those provided by the National Science Foundation) or special endowment funds.[3] At least three of the colleges are either now engaged in, or have projected, fund-raising efforts for the support of their graduate studies. And a number of church-related colleges continue to rely upon church contributions either in the form of annual grants earmarked for this purpose (six only) or contributed services from the clerical faculty (12 colleges).

The internal sources of support, however, are the ones with which a majority of the institutions must concern themselves and from which many of the inherent dangers emanate. Thirty-eight colleges report that they are totally reliant upon income from graduate student fees to carry the cost of the program. At the other end of the scale, only two institutions indicate that no fees are paid directly by their graduate students (this does not include those for whom the fees are paid by employers or by the supporting religious bodies).

Occasionally the summer graduate enrollment is sufficiently extensive to subsidize the costs of the much more limited activities conducted during the regular academic year. Elsewhere—and this is very likely more prevalent than the reports would indicate—the undergraduate program, which profits indirectly from the presence of graduate students on the campus, is expected to provide some subsidy (ranging

3. One college reports an endowment of $600,000, another of $327,000, for the exclusive use of the graduate program. A third indicates annual contributions from "friends" of $38,000 to $50,000 for graduate studies.

from an estimated ten to seventy-five per cent). This is sometimes done directly; at other times, indirectly through a kind of budgetary legerdemain in which either no instructional or institutional overhead, or a minimal amount thereof, is charged against the graduate program.

To the specific question of overhead charges, 34 colleges replied that the graduate school carried its full share of overhead, based on proportional enrollment or proportional income from fees and other sources. Thirty-three colleges indicated that the graduate programs, even though they might be more expensive to operate, carry a lower percentage of the institutional overhead than the undergraduate. Another 38 either failed to answer the question at all or indicated that no answer was possible.

The reason for this last is, of course, the difficulty in the type of institution included in this survey—or for that matter in even the more complex universities—of determining just what cost can rightly be allocated to the graduate program. Where completely separate facilities and/or equipment are provided, a differentiation is easy (this was true with only two colleges, both denominational and both serving a highly specialized function); but, as will be discussed shortly, the maintenance of separate facilities is the exception, not the rule. And how about library facilities and resources? Even though some institutions have a separate budget item for the graduate library acquisitions, the books and other research resources are certainly available to both graduate and undergraduate alike. Where graduate scholarships and assistantships are provided, here too the problem is relatively simple. But, at least with the latter, the assistant's stipend and tuition could, with some logic, be charged to either the graduate or the undergraduate budget. As for the faculty, here the complexities are manifold. Simply to allocate costs on the basis of the actual credit hours of divided time is unrealistic if, as should be the case, graduate preparation and counseling responsibilities are more demanding than the undergraduate.

The complexities of this problem of overhead charges are well described in the following reply from a leading Eastern institution:

A distinction must be made between the graduate program in the academic year and that in the summer.

1. During the academic year there is no charge made for overhead because graduate students are largely taught in advanced undergradu-

ate courses and, until this year, no load credit has been given for guidance of M.A. theses (we will henceforth grant such credit, probably four theses as equal to one course, with credit accumulated). Aside from a quarter salary for the director and the full tuition and stipend paid the preceptors, cost of graduate work to the University has been part-time secretarial assistance. Beyond these costs, the income from graduate work has been absorbed in the undergraduate budget and, thereby, contributed in the same proportion to overhead.

2. The Summer Session covers full direct costs plus the indirect costs for the facilities used (which means about 50% of the total overhead in the summer period involved).

Implicit in this description is the fact that the graduate programs, as they mature, manifest an upward trend in costs which may or may not be paralleled in income. To maintain a viable program the support must obviously come from one or a combination of three sources: the general income of the undergraduate program, graduate school fees, or outside grants or subsidies. As has been said, the differences in budgetary practices make reliable statistical presentation difficult. Nevertheless, an interesting picture of the distribution of such support is given in Table 30, which is based upon estimates provided by 110 of the colleges included in this study.

TABLE 30

Sources of Financial Support for Graduate Programs in 98 Colleges

(Data Based on Questionnaires)

	0%	1-25%	26-50%	51-75%	76-100%	Percentage Unspecified
The Undergraduate Program	5	8	9	4	1	22
Graduate Fees	3	4	14	8	27	31
Outside Subsidy	2	6	15	3	7	24

Looking at the problem of total financial resources for the maintenance of a viable graduate school, one gets an insight into both the problems and prospects of one of the more vigorous programs from the following brief comment:

The development of the . . . program has been hampered by the lack of money to provide fellowships, to expand the number of students, to build up the library and, above all, to maintain a genuine graduate faculty and curriculum. The summer program, however, may prove a source of support which could buttress the graduate offerings in the regular academic year. If to this could be added adequate support from the . . . Foundation, our program of graduate studies could contribute much to the initial graduate education of the scholar-teacher for the colleges as well as for the secondary schools.

Its problems are soluble; its potentialities not inconsiderable.

An equally difficult problem in obtaining definitive information for this study was that concerning facilities. For, except where the graduate program was designed to meet a highly specialized need—as, for example, a program in museum education—a majority of the graduate programs seem to share facilities in common with the undergraduate program. Seventy-seven of the colleges indicate that they have not added any new facilities to accommodate their graduate work. The remaining 66 have made at least a minimal recognition of their graduate study through the provision of added facilities or equipment.

The most common addition was to the library. Fifty colleges reported substantial improvements to their library buildings and collections within the past decade as a direct result of meeting their graduate needs. Three of these have built totally new library buildings, taking into account their graduate offerings in developing their building plans.

The replies to the question "To what extent was your library budget increased to meet the needs of the graduate program?" reflected, perhaps as much as anything else, the varied patterns of library budgeting. A number of colleges indicated that vigorous steps were taken at the outset of their programs to remedy deficiencies in their collections in the graduate areas. At one college, for example, an initial outlay of $15,000 was made for education and another $9,000 for business. Thereafter, for a period of nine years, these areas received $2,000 and $3,000 for annual acquisitions. A similar departmental pattern is seen in a half dozen other colleges.

On the other hand, some of the respondents indicated that a special graduate allocation, without departmental significance, is added to the undergraduate library budget. At one college this amounts to an annual $3,500 in a budget of $26,000; in another, $5,000 in a total budget of $50,000 per year. Such subsidies as are represented by the National Science Foundation or National Defense Education Act[4] summer institutes provide funds earmarked for library acquisitions in areas covered by the grant. Only two colleges reported requiring a library fee of their graduate students to assist in strengthening their library holdings.

The most common reply to the question, however, was that no distinction is made between the graduate and the undergraduate programs in budgeting for the library—this despite the harsh economic fact that an adequate library service for a quality graduate program is considered to cost three to four times the amount needed for undergraduate programs in most subject fields. Nevertheless, some of the colleges were able to point to the fact that their library holdings had increased substantially since the inauguration of graduate work. In one instance they doubled and in another they reportedly tripled. It is significant, though, that 67 of the respondents specified improvement of the library as one of the most essential needs if their graduate program is to develop in quality.

As for other facilities, 15 colleges report added laboratories to accommodate their graduate programs in science and language; and a few have added classrooms (ten colleges) and seminar rooms (seven). A few colleges have established separate graduate school offices; one boasts of a graduate room for its students; and one has leased housing for graduate students. The overwhelming majority of the colleges, however, indicate that no new facilities have been added as a result of their graduate programs. They further state that none of their facilities are reserved exclusively for the use of graduate students, with the exception of a few colleges which provide library carrels and some laboratory space for research (with the latter usually being shared by the faculty).

4. While technically the provision for language and area centers under Section 601(a) of Title VI is open to institutions offering only the M.A., for the most part grants have been limited to institutions offering the Ph.D. Research and study programs under Section 602 are also available to the smaller college, particularly those developing MAT programs "with foreign language teaching implications." The report on the first two years of the program, however, did not indicate grants to any of the institutions among the 143 included in this study.

When asked what additional facilities would be helpful in the further development of their programs, nearly one-third of the colleges offered no replies, presumably indicating a general satisfaction with present facilities. From those which did respond the most common needs, aside from improved library resources, were for laboratory facilities (25), student housing (9), classrooms and seminar rooms (7 each), study facilities (6), counseling facilities (6), curriculum laboratories (4), a training school for teachers (3), a reading clinic (3), and faculty offices (2).

The conclusion seems almost inescapable at this point that the majority of the colleges included in this study are making no substantial capital investment in their graduate programs. Only one college, in fact, indicates that it has a separate building for its graduate school, a building formerly occupied by an academy which was operated under college sponsorship. Two others indicate that, in moving onto new campuses, they gave some thought to the accommodation of their graduate programs. As for the rest, the observation made by one of the respondents, in another context, would probably hold true here: "It is difficult to identify any reductions of overhead which could be realized if the graduate program were to be abolished."[5]

5. Specific guidelines for evolving a graduate budget were considered to be beyond the scope of this study. Nevertheless, the following books, several of which are probably on every financial officer's desk, contain many useful aids: *College and University Business Administration*, Vols. I and II (Washington: American Council on Education, 1952, 1955); *Financing Higher Education: 1960-70* (New York: McGraw-Hill Book Company, Inc., 1959); Thad L. Hungate, *Finance in Educational Management of Colleges and Universities* (New York: Bureau of Publications, Teachers College, Columbia University, 1954); John D. Millett, *Financing Higher Education in the United States* (New York: Columbia University Press, 1952); William H. Roe, *School Business Management* (New York: McGraw-Hill Book Company, Inc., 1962); Clarence Scheps, *Accounting for Colleges and Universities* (Baton Rouge, La.: Louisiana State University Press, 1949).

CHAPTER VIII

The Pros and Cons

The private liberal arts college which is seriously contemplating entering the field of graduate study will find encouragement, if not inspiration, in the fact that those now engaged, when asked to list the advantages and disadvantages of their involvement, reported an overwhelming preponderance of advantages. This was true in the replies received from the officials responsible for the programs. It was even more true in the replies from the random sampling of participating faculty members. Such favorable response may, of course, merely reflect the characteristic optimism of *homo academiensus*. Or, another possibility, it may indicate merely that the private college, having had the courage to enter the graduate field, has perforce convinced itself that its role in this academic drama is one of significance.

The purpose of this chapter is to present the advantages and disadvantages as seen by those colleges now engaged in offering graduate study, without any distinction being drawn among the various types of graduate programs. And while many of the advantages suggest antithetical disadvantages, the plan of this chapter will be to present the pros and cons separately. An implicit evaluation is made in Chapter IX, which is devoted to specific suggestions and recommendations.

Although the expressed advantages cover a vast range, they are, for purposes of this discussion, grouped under the two principal categories of *external* and *internal* advantages. It need hardly be said that this distinction is artificial, for nearly any advantage accruing to the one must, directly or indirectly, accrue to the other.

Regardless of other objectives, nearly every college which has offered graduate study, as we discussed in Chapter I, was motivated by a desire to provide some form of service, a service which, in the opinion of the institution, it was peculiarly equipped to perform. For example, one respondent makes the following observation: "From the viewpoint of a private church-related college the graduate program offers a number of distinct advantages. It gives opportunity for emphasis on a distinctly Christian philosophy in the training of teachers and other personnel, many of whom will enter or continue in church-related activities." Thus, several of the colleges emphasize the desirability of being able to devote attention to the promulgation of religious concepts or, more generally, to character development. The assumption here, of course, is that the larger, more impersonal graduate school is not in a position to provide a similar emphasis. Moreover, since some of the graduate programs are devoted almost exclusively to meeting certain parochial needs, the following statement is doubtless applicable in more than one school: "More of our own Sisters can continue in graduate work at less cost to the Community."

In this area of service, nearly 70 institutions emphasized the value of their services to both the teachers and the schools in their geographical area. One college, for example, with some justification, boasted of the impact which it has had in the raising of the level of education in Southern Negro schools. Over fifty per cent of the public school principals in the major city in which it is located received their master's training from that college. Through the preparation of administrators, teachers, and specialists a college can exert a tremendous amount of leadership on the school systems in its vicinity. The same, of course, can be said of the large university. But the proponents of the liberal arts concept feel that their emphasis upon liberal training is peculiarly beneficial. Thus, even where the college has competition with nearby teacher-training institutions, there is considered to be a beneficial missionary value in providing education courses in a liberal arts frame of reference.

Where there are no other facilities in the immediate area, the private college rightfully believes that it performs a valuable service in providing a means for continued education for those elementary and secondary school teachers who might not be able to travel the distances involved in going to the nearest university. Such service is not limited, of course, to the public schools. As we have implied, some of the colleges devote special attention to the preparation of teachers for parochial schools. At least two of the respondents emphasized that their graduate programs have provided a means whereby secondary school teachers have prepared for, and subsequently entered, the field of college teaching. And, of course, there are already a few colleges in the group which have developed master's programs for the preparation of teachers for junior colleges.

Before leaving the subject of services to teaching, it is important to point out, as several of the respondents did in their replies, that the institution itself benefits considerably from the "public relations potential" of having master teachers who can influence high school students in their choice of college. Moreover, to the extent that the college improves the quality of instruction in its "feeder" secondary schools, to that extent it can benefit from the improved quality of the students entering its freshman class.

There are other forms of community service as well which a college can provide through graduate study. In particular, some have found benefit in serving local industry which needs graduate courses both to attract and to develop technical and managerial personnel. Here too the service is a two-way street, for the resultant improvement and enlargement of the institution's sphere of influence frequently results in improved financial support. Thus a number of the colleges emphasized the gains in prestige and recognition which reportedly eventuated from their provision of graduate work of high quality. (Parenthetically, one of the respondents felt that the school benefited substantially from the fact that, by offering graduate study for clergymen, it gained many friends and wider support from the controlling church organization.) In fact, at least three of the institutions indicated that they consider their graduate programs as playing a focal role in community-wide efforts to provide leadership for general economic and culture improvement in the area.

Clearly, in the foregoing no sharp distinction has been drawn between the advantages which the college itself can receive and the benefits it can provide to the community it serves through the maintenance of a good graduate program. A similar duality is inevitable in discussing the advantages in terms of the faculty.

The faculty member himself profits in many ways from a graduate program. As a number of respondents observed, the teacher experiences an uplift to that much-discussed entity in academic circles, his morale, when he is able to devote at least a portion of his time to students for whom academic work is not a matter of secondary importance. One reply indicated that the faculty participants in the graduate program were "happier and more contented." An administrator might look long for a stronger incentive for the introduction of a graduate program! There can be little doubt, however, that working with graduate students who have a genuine interest in the subject provides a degree of stimulus not available in the average classroom with the average undergraduate. Thus it is that a number of the replies from both faculty and administration suggested that the instructor "is brought alive" through involvement in graduate teaching. One aspect of this boosting of morale, reportedly, comes when a faculty member trains a master's candidate who is accepted for doctoral study in one of the major universities. It is not often in the life of a teacher that such tangible results are so readily discernible.

The fact that 35 of the questionnaires emphasized the importance of faculty stimulation justifies giving this subject additional attention. As was pointed out in many of the replies, this stimulation comes not only from the presence of more dedicated students in the classroom, but also from certain other opportunities which may not be quite so prevalent in the institution where instruction is limited to undergraduate work. One of the respondents, in claiming certain advantages for the liberal arts college over the university, writes:

> In a smaller college, the different departments and academic discipline may have more contacts with one another. I have an idea that there is more mutual discussion and criticism of ideas when faculty members are more likely to know members in fields of study different from their own.

A refinement of this idea is the beneficial effect of the presence of one or two specialists, especially engaged for graduate courses, on other members of the faculty. Seven colleges, in fact, made observations on the desirability of having these scholars on the campus.

On the other side of this same coin, there is evidence that the development of a graduate program stimulates the faculty member to greater communication with colleagues on the same level at other institutions. The assumption here is that it is much more difficult for the faculty to remain insular if it is involved in graduate study. One need scarcely add that these observations present a kind of indictment of the undergraduate instruction in a great many colleges. But, as one respondent, in a very revealing remark, stated: "The principal limitation at this college is the tradition of complacency and mediocrity in the faculty: graduate work presupposes good men to promote it." There is a prevailing feeling in many of the reports that the presence of the graduate program encourages the faculty members to prepare more carefully, to conduct independent study, and to become engaged in productive research. This research may actually be somewhat vicarious in that it may involve only the direction of graduate theses. But, as one instructor sagely observed, the very act of reading a graduate thesis, "though time consuming, is beneficial for the faculty member."

There can be little doubt that the presence of a graduate program of substantial proportion enables the institution to engage the services of scholars with a greater degree of specialization than would ordinarily be required for undergraduate teaching. Moreover, there can be little doubt that, as was pointed out in one of the questionnaires, "there are persons who really do better work in the quiet of a small college than in the competitive atmosphere of a large university." For such persons, "the teaching of a graduate course or two keeps alive an interest in their particular field, makes them keep alert to the current scholarship, and may even stimulate them to go on with their own research."

An important stimulus to any such personal research is the presence on the campus of qualified graduate or research assistants. Thus some 13 of the colleges stressed the importance of the graduate program in providing the faculty member with highly qualified aides. These young persons may either assist in research or take over some of the other duties of the faculty member to free him for personal research. Thus another 15 institutions emphasized the benefits to the faculty of having skilled assistants in laboratory courses.

On the positive side it can be claimed that a graduate program enables a private college to attract faculty members of the quality that might not otherwise be available to it. On the negative side, many liberal arts colleges will find it increasingly difficult to hold the top young professors if there are no opportunities for the type of research and the level of instruction generally implicit in a graduate program.

But there is still another relevant point to be made here, and this has to do with the small liberal arts college versus the large university. Not many years ago a substantial percentage of the nation's college teachers received their undergraduate training, and presumably discovered their interest in college teaching, in the independent liberal arts college. Many of these persons, even though they went on to the larger universities for advanced study, retained their sympathetic interest in the small college.[1] More recently, however, there has been a change in the undergraduate origins of our college teachers. More of them are now graduates of large universities. Moreover, they are graduates of public, tax-supported institutions. These new recruits to the teaching profession can scarcely be expected to have much understanding of, or sympathy for, independent liberal arts colleges. Thus it might well be considered a matter of ultimate survival for the colleges to devote time and thought to the preparation of young men and women for careers in college teaching, and more specifically for teaching careers in the type of college in which they found satisfaction as students, both undergraduate and graduate.

And, is it not equally important that there should be a maximum interchange between different types of institutions in training teachers for each other, if higher education is to preserve its essential unity? If so—and it surely is so—then does not the independent liberal arts college have an obligation to hold up its end in this process of exchange?

In discussing the advantages of the graduate program in the independent college in terms of faculty, there were implicit certain advantages also in terms of the graduate students. To look now more specifically at the student himself, a number of the better liberal arts colleges consider it one of their primary functions to provide an intermediate stage for the college graduate of ability who is not quite ready to participate in the more intensive doctoral programs in the larger graduate schools. The student may be the "late bloomer," who did not find himself academically until near the close of his baccalaureate program. This can be interpreted in several ways. First, it can refer to the student who did not particularly apply himself and thus did not achieve the average which would qualify him for admis-

1. See Allan O. Pfnister, *A Report on the Baccalaureate Origins of College Faculties* (Washington: Association of American Colleges, 1961).

sion to the more competitive graduate schools. Or, second, it can apply to the student who, though superior academically, has serious deficiencies in his background. These may, for example, be deficiencies in foreign languages or other "tool" subjects; or they may result from a late change in field of concentration with consequent deficiencies in certain courses prerequisite to the intensive doctoral curriculum. Thus the master's program in the smaller college can be considered a kind of way station toward the Ph.D.

But these are not the only types of students who find the presence of a master's program in the smaller college advantageous. In a number of institutions, for example, the more capable undergraduates are able to combine work in their upper years with actual graduate study in which they earn credits towards the master's degree. Moreover, the movement toward the three-year master's program, in which are combined the last two years of the baccalaureate with one full year of master's study, may well have received a very strong impetus from the recent publication of Dr. Carmichael's provocative book *Graduate Education*.[2] The stimulus to the better undergraduate student provided by such a program is undoubtedly a strong argument in favor of the liberal arts college entering the field of graduate study.

But even where there is no such formal program for coordinating undergraduate and graduate work, the undergraduate may still benefit from the presence of graduate students on the campus. He can do so indirectly because of the stimulus to his instructors, which was discussed earlier. He can do so through the opportunity to have contacts with more mature students who are carrying on advanced study and research in his immediate vicinity—a greater possibility on the small than on the large campus. By taking classes with graduate students he can find both inspiration and challenge in their very presence, a potential advantage which was discussed by a score of respondents.

But to return to the graduate student, at least the full-time student has a greater chance to become a part of the total college community in a small college than he would have in the large university. Thus, for the teacher seeking to upgrade himself by obtaining a master's degree, the opportunity to take courses on the compact campus has a distinct edge over the off-campus extension courses which have become preva-

2. *Graduate Education: A Critique and a Program* (New York: Harper & Brothers, 1961), pp. 162-77.

lent in many areas. Among other things, he has the benefit of utilizing the college library resources and of closer contact with faculty members. And, of course, the very availability of graduate study within easy geographical reach provides an added incentive for him to advance himself academically and professionally. And, finally, he may receive more intimate guidance than would be available in the larger, more impersonal setting.

For the student who is not planning to go beyond the master's level, there may well be a particular advantage in his attending the college where greater attention is given to work at this level. A vigorous case for this point of view was made by one of the directors of a small graduate program, who wrote as follows:

> The degree itself is good; it is a respectable and useful stage in the scholarly hierarchy. The improvement which it needs is public acceptance of its respectability. This can come only from good colleges providing good master's programs. The Ph.D. granting institutions have degraded the degree and will never reestablish it. In my opinion this is one of the best contributions which the small private liberal arts colleges can make to American education.

Another writer, in making somewhat the same point, suggested that the large universities discontinue the master's degree altogether in the belief that it could flourish better in the fertile soil of the small campus!

The ability to attract and hold faculty members whose experience and training fit them for teaching graduate courses and the presence on the campus of both part-time and full-time students who are more mature and dedicated than the average undergraduate are among the most attractive reasons for the maintenance of graduate programs in the independent college. These two factors combine, moreover, to make possible an enrichment of the curriculum to the benefit of both undergraduate and graduate students. At the same time they provide a strong incentive for raising the academic standards on all levels.

A number of the colleges commented on the value of the intensive curricular studies which were made at the inauguration of their graduate programs and which, either with or without stimulation from the regional accrediting bodies, encourage periodic self-evaluation. The claim is that the graduate program requires more intensive and more frequent evaluation. The observation is also made that the graduate programs in the smaller institutions provide for much more departmental cross-fertilization than is generally possible in the larger graduate school setting. Moreover, a number of the colleges emphasized the beneficial effects of having the faculty members or chairmen of their graduate departments working closely with their counterparts in neighboring graduate schools, whether or not a formal relationship between the two institutions exists, as it does in a number of colleges. In a few, for example, the cooperating university actually conducts graduate work on the college campus, either during the summer only or throughout the academic year. In the instruction of these courses faculty members of both institutions may cooperate to the consequent enrichment of the smaller institution.

As is evident in the chapter on Standards and Curriculum, a number of the colleges are providing graduate sequences based on an integrated curriculum rather than on the high degree of specialization generally characteristic of the larger graduate schools. These programs are particularly advantageous for the elementary or secondary school teacher whose academic background may not have provided the necessary degree of liberal or general training. Other colleges, on the contrary, provide programs which allow for what they consider a salutary degree of specialization not generally possible in an undergraduate curriculum. For example, one in this group developed an outstanding summer program of graduate training in foreign languages which even includes formal study abroad. Other colleges have been able to offer summer institutes in the sciences and mathematics, through government subsidy, which have brought to the campus many persons of ability and which, at the same time, have provided a valuable stimulus to their own faculty.

Since in a majority of the colleges the graduate courses are actually extensions of the undergraduate curriculum—the difference being one of depth—there is generally considered to be a beneficial feedback. This is particularly true where the courses are combined and where the instructor, as a consequence, maintains a high degree of expectation from each level of student.

Finally, from the standpoint of the faculty at least, one of the greatest advantages of the graduate program consists in the professors' being able to offer, even if only occasionally, highly specialized courses in areas of their particular interest to students of better than average competence. Moreover, they have the opportunity to employ the graduate seminar method, which permits a degree of concentration not ordinarily possible in their undergraduate labors. Summing this up, one of the faculty respondents writes:

> To the extent that graduate education should and must be "tailor-made" and suited to the particular needs of the individual student within the framework of an established set of standards, the small liberal arts college has inherent advantages over relatively larger colleges and universities. Small liberal arts colleges are likely to be in a position to offer personalized services which would encourage broader and more profound development than might be possible in a large, impersonal, highly specialized institution which employs "production line" techniques.

The number is admittedly small, but some of the colleges nevertheless claim certain financial advantages in the maintenance of the graduate program. A few, for example, have been able to attract funds to set up endowed chairs for graduate instruction. Others have attracted funds for graduate fellowships and assistantships and, in a subsidized program, amounts have generally been available to provide some additions to instructional equipment and facilities. A substantial number of the institutions commented favorably on the library improvements which have come about as a direct result of their graduate programs. Even though these library improvements may be limited to specific fields, they nevertheless represent an upgrading of the library as an instructional tool. A number of the colleges, moreover, observed that their graduate courses, held as they are in the late afternoon or in the summer, make possible a fuller utilization of the plant and thereby contribute to the institution's over-all financial stability.

Although this catalogue of advantages could be continued, it will be closed on one final note that was struck in a number of the questionnaires. For one of the strongest advantages, though perhaps the most difficult to define, seems to be the fact that the graduate programs represent an important status symbol both within the institution and among its constituency. This is variously expressed as a "general improvement in the colleges' public relations," "a better understanding of the role of the college among high school teachers and administrators," or "improvement of our reputation for high-level perform-ance."

At what price this status may be gained can, perhaps, be best evaluated by looking next at some of the reported disadvantages accru-ing to the independent liberal arts college which maintains a graduate program.

Disadvantages. It is ironical, and yet understandable, that virtually every advantage has its counterpart on the opposite side of the ledger. Despite the similarities which many of these colleges share, they cover a wide enough range in resources, capacities, and geographical op-portunities to present a variety of approaches to the question of graduate study.

Practically no institution, however, suggested that the task of the central administration is rendered any easier by the presence of a graduate program, except the ability of the institution to attract more and perhaps better faculty members. In fact, high on the list of dis-advantages are the additional burdens assumed by one or more of the chief administrative officers. Despite need for a full-time director of the graduate program, as was indicated in Chapter III, a vast majority of the colleges in this group assign the task to a member of the staff, usually the dean, who is already weighed down with other duties. One result is that, instead of finding time for the encouragement of "intellectual virtues," he has to concentrate upon rules and regulations, schedules and examinations, even recruitment and dismissals. Thus, he cannot but feel, as many of the respondents evidently do, that the graduate programs interfere not only with his primary interests but with the main objectives of the college as a whole.

He discovers on many campuses that the percentage of part-time students among the graduate complement raises the difficulty of sched-uling courses at hours when they might be attractive to some of the better students from the advanced undergraduate body. He finds that the classes in the late afternoons and on Saturday morning tend to be looked upon as a separate activity, with the consequence that the graduate program, which could exercise a beneficial effect upon the campus as a whole, has an almost imperceptible impact. He feels a sense of frustration in that the master's degree, which under the best circumstances should lead toward the doctorate, is for many of his students the end of their formal academic aspirations. Moreover, he sees that the burden of the graduate program tends to rest most heavily on relatively few departments, often upon those which potentially could make the greatest contribution to the main purpose of the campus—the education of the undergraduate. Instead, they become overextended and thus less effectual. The temptation to undertake too much is ever present, and he finds himself obliged to frustrate the aspirations of some of his more ambitious colleagues.

Another danger to which he must be constantly alert is "a subtle but pervasive temptation to be satisfied with the *status quo*." In other words, once departments have expended some of their creative energies on the development of graduate programs, they tend to become content "with being fairly sizable frogs in small ponds," whereas a constant and candid comparison with the faculty and student body in comparable departments in the more prestigious institutions would show much that actually is wanting. At times, of course, the difference is brought home rather embarrassingly when some of the graduate students run into difficulty having courses accepted for transfer credit. This difficulty may be further accentuated when the college develops a graduate program that is somewhat different from the more conventional offerings elsewhere.

Even where his program begins with strong support from local industry, he may discover, as one dean did, the following situation:

> Industry has a tendency to "use" a program. After claiming a great need for a particular course, the industrialist will lament its cancellation if only two or three register. The quality of the work performed is of a much higher caliber than in some of our sister institutions. When we insist on retaining this quality, we lose numerically to these other schools.

In other words, although smallness may in some areas be a virtue, in the graduate area this virtue may be bought at a heavy price—a price that is paid often by the director of the program, if not by the total undergraduate school as well.

But the price is also paid by the members of the faculty, including departmental chairmen, who often have to spend an inordinate amount of time recruiting graduate students. Once recruited, the students may require a greater degree of tutorial direction than would seem to be desirable from the standpoint of the chairman's total obligations.

As for the faculty member, the satisfactions derived from teaching graduate students—or to put this in another way, the status which this activity may give him in the eyes of his colleagues both on and off the campus—may not adequately compensate him for the additional hardships which he experiences, particularly when the graduate courses are allocated an insufficient amount of time or when they are over and above his normal work load. In fact, the most common complaint from the faculty members related to what many of them consider a heavy demand upon their time without due consideration. Even where the graduate courses are part of the normal teaching load, very often the supervision of theses and the participation in oral examinations are not so accounted.

As was evident earlier in this report, there are still other frustrations for the faculty member. Graduate teaching requires what to many appears to be an undue effort for a relatively small number of students. Further, many of the students are not, in the ideal sense of the term, graduate students at all. Many of them are persons who could not qualify for admission in the better graduate schools. Others are mere shoppers, with only limited motivation to buy, an attitude not limited to any particular class of graduate school.

But there are two other frustrations which an occasional faculty member considered to be even more severe. The first of these is that there are not, among his colleagues, even among those teaching graduate courses, many whom he might consider truly graduate teachers. They do not feel the usual stimulus to research, the *sine qua non* of the graduate instructor, even if the stimulus may be the rather negative "publish or perish." Thus, he may feel that the courses which parallel his could be better characterized as advanced undergraduate than as graduate courses in any strict sense. And finally he may discover that support for his own research is more difficult to obtain in the limited, relatively unknown, graduate program than it would be if he were associated with a more prestigious graduate school.

The observation has already been made that the quality of students in many of the graduate programs leaves something to be desired. It should be added here that these are not limited to the less-known schools. In fact, several of the reporting colleges (including one of the outstanding colleges in the country) indicate that, particularly since they do not encourage their own graduates to continue on the campus, they have real difficulty in attracting students of superior talent into their master's program. The candid observation is made that "students holding A.B. degrees from . . . or its equivalent should probably go at once to a university for graduate work."

In many of the schools the serious student may run into some of the frustrations reported by the graduate teacher. For example, because of the relatively small number of graduate students in his courses, or in the school as a whole, he may well find little of the stimulation of competition characteristic of the larger graduate departments. He will also find, in a majority of the colleges, a substantial percentage of part-time students; and this creates the situation described in the following:

> In many cases, M.A. students who are drawn from the community, represent people holding full-time jobs who wish gradually to take credits toward a degree. This makes the M.A. program a course-by-course, credit-by-credit pursuit, with little real commitment.

Even when there is a small complement of full-time graduate students, these are often busily engaged as teaching fellows or laboratory assistants who have surprisingly little direct contact one with the other. If the reports are correct, there is limited social intercourse among the graduate students in the smaller colleges, possibly because of the absence of dormitory facilities or other meeting rooms where they might naturally congregate for intellectual and social interchange.

But this may be the least of the ills. For in the small college the graduate student may have less opportunity to meet some of the "greats" in the field of his academic interest. While there may indeed be one or two outstanding faculty members, the private liberal arts college probably cannot provide this luxury in abundance. Therefore, the graduate student may find himself exposed to a much narrower range of ideas and miss the excitement which comes from direct encounters with some of the leaders in the field.

Moreover, he may find himself enrolled in a program which is merely an adjunct to the undergraduate program, and not truly of graduate quality or focus. This can be reflected in both content and methodology. Many of the courses which should be strictly graduate level are still "textbook" courses; and the graduate student, who should be making independent explorations into relatively uncharted waters, may find himself directed in a manner detrimental to his best interests.

Because of the limited facilities for research in both the library and laboratory, and perhaps also because of his own limited time if he is fully employed elsewhere, such explorations may be out of the question.

In fact, the weaknesses of the curriculum and of the facilities for research are among the most commonly presented disadvantages in the small college programs. The inability to offer a broad program, particularly a program which lacks supporting graduate courses in other departments, is a serious drawback to the designing of a meaningful sequence. A graduate curriculum in physics quite obviously must be sustained by adequate courses in mathematics. Perhaps a little less obviously, a graduate program in English should be sustained by graduate courses in history and philosophy. But in many of the smaller colleges any such extension would represent a dangerous proliferation. Instead, what frequently happens is that the extension is achieved through permitting the graduate student to elect undergraduate courses, in which he may not necessarily receive the desired level of instruction. Further, there is a strong tendency "to slump to undergraduate standards" in this all too common integration of the two levels.

In the opinion of many of the persons who were interviewed in the process of this study, the greatest weakness in the master's programs in the liberal arts colleges is the absence of "intellectual crossbreeding" on the graduate school level. So long as the fields of specialization remain too few and too narrow, there can be little hope of a change for the better. Nearly one-third of the colleges view this as a weakness of their own programs and as a general disadvantage in the master's programs in relatively small institutions.

In short, the programs tend to be oriented not so much for the graduate student but for the benefit of the college itself. Thus many of the programs lack a distinctive identity. They tend to be utilitarian and technical rather than to place emphasis upon the acquisition or the advancement of knowledge for its own sake (an all too common fault in many of the larger graduate schools as well).

Even in the programs limited to the preparation of secondary school teachers these dangers are by no means absent. As one respondent pointed out, "if the graduate program contains nothing but education courses, there is no general value to the college, just a general lowering of the entire tone of the campus to professionalism." Many of the colleges make some effort to correct this imbalance by permitting graduate students to take undergraduate subjects for advanced credit, but this is a practice which can scarcely be greeted with enthusiasm by those who feel that the independent college has a real contribution to make in the area of graduate study.

It is undoubtedly true that one of the principal ingredients missing in the graduate programs in private liberal arts colleges is a sufficient amount of financial seasoning. The addition of graduate study merely tends to compound the difficulty. Thus a number of the respondents admitted that their general budget was not adequate to enable them to conduct programs of the quality that they might desire. Higher faculty salaries are necessary to attract teachers of top quality; and, as one dean observed, "a small college must offer high paying scholarships to attract good graduate students, giving money in place of prestige." Nevertheless, it is obvious that relatively few of the colleges are in condition to offer grants matching those available to the better students in the wealthier universities. Any effort to compete dollar for dollar would be generally at the expense of the undergraduate program, particularly since outside grants are difficult to obtain. Moreover, to attract better graduate students, and more full-time students, housing should be made available on the campus. The library should be substantially increased and, along with this, other facilities for study and research should be provided. There should even, for certain subjects, be segregated collections in the library; and a discussion and social area could well be set aside for graduate students. And yet all of this requires a much greater expenditure than can ordinarily be justified.

Therefore, the hazards of graduate study, as reported by those responsible for its conduct and even by some of the students seeking graduate degrees in these colleges, are such as to make it desirable for any administrator or faculty committee to walk very warily indeed.

But—to give this chapter an *aria da capo* movement—the need for graduate opportunities is expanding at an alarming rate. Already many independently structured colleges are doing an outstanding job, better in fact than many of the universities, on the master's level. Therefore, it would almost be irresponsible for the liberal arts college to ignore the need or to fail to make a realistic assessment of its possible role in this growing extension of American higher education.

CHAPTER IX

Some Advice, Exhortation, and Expostulation

The final question on the basic questionnaire [1] used to elicit information for this study reads as follows: "What general advice would you
give a similar institution contemplating the inauguration of a graduate
program?"

Of all the replies to this question, the most succinct and emotionally
charged came from the dean of a liberal arts college in the South. It
consisted of the single word, "Don't!" At the other end of the scale,
the academic dean of one of the better liberal arts colleges in the Midwest wrote, "I think most institutions of our size should have a selective
program with the M.A. degree as the terminal degree." Between these
two views, the replies contained a wealth of advice which, blended
with the reflections of the authors over their two-year study, provide
the substance of this final chapter.

As was noted in Chapter VIII, there are many good reasons why
the private liberal arts college should inaugurate and maintain a graduate program. There are also many good reasons for scaling a mountain peak. But neither of these activities should be engaged in light-
heartedly. What is needed for each, reportedly, is a well-conceived
plan, followed by a strong measure of common sense, patience, and
endurance.

1.   Questionnaire "B." See Appendix II.

The first essential for the college contemplating graduate study is to make a careful short- and long-range analysis of both the external and internal variables intrinsic to any such undertaking. As we noted earlier in this report, one college protracted its study over a ten-year period before actually enrolling the first graduate student. The proximity of other graduate opportunities is certainly a matter of concern in any such evaluation. Their presence does not necessarily rule out a new undertaking, but "the recognized excellence of one institution over another in certain limited fields should be respected and programs be instituted which avoid overlapping."

While respecting the piety in this advice, one must also grant that it has practical applicability. For despite the increasing demand for graduate work, the institution entering the field, particularly if there are other programs within commuting distance, will find itself up against the type of competition which can best be met by a distinctive, if not unique, approach to graduate instruction. The colleges which have developed the most successful programs in recent years are those which have made a careful survey of the need for the types of offerings which they wish to project. Unless this survey shows that a college is in a position to provide a real service to the community, near and far, it would obviously do well to stick to its undergraduate last.

The techniques of making such external surveys, while varied, are sufficiently accessible to need no elaboration here. Nevertheless, a number of colleges have sought professional counsel for both this phase of the study and for the more intricate phase of internal evaluation.[2] In this latter, the answers to the questionnaires emphasize strongly the desirability of first reviewing carefully the institution's traditional objectives. Because a small graduate program ordinarily requires sacrifices on the part of both faculty and administration, it should certainly not be undertaken if it involves so basic a change in the philosophy of the institution that the larger mass of undergraduate students may be deprived of any part of their rightful heritage.

In fact, no college should begin graduate study unless it can point to a strong undergraduate program, not just in a few departments but consistently throughout. This does not imply, incidentally, that all of

2. Several of the regional accrediting associations, as was indicated in Chapter II, have provided useful guides for making internal evaluations of the capacity for, or quality of, graduate programs. Pertinent extracts from these guides are reproduced in Appendix IV.

the outstanding departments should rush pell-mell into master's programs, despite the fact that the more aggressive chairmen will probably seek to do so. The questionnaires contained many interesting words of advice on this subject. For the most part, there was agreement with the following: "Limit the work to a few departments; give these departments adequate staffing; require of them a high level of performance."

Even within the departments there should not necessarily be any carte blanche. For example, in political science, it might be well to limit the master's program to international relations, excluding the other traditional areas of interest within that field. Some of the correspondents recommended developing traditional fields first; others indicated that the science department should be the first to undertake graduate study; still others, that the first program should be in the field of professional education. The best advice, however, would be for the college to evaluate its external demands and internal capacities and, on the basis of the findings, begin drilling where there is the best prospect of striking oil. In particular, there should be stronger reason for determining what will be offered than a desire on the part of a few faculty members to teach graduate courses or on the part of some students to accumulate graduate credits.

"Granted the need for the program," one writer indicates, "the next step is to develop faith, hope, and patience." These qualities are essential for a variety of reasons, some obvious, some not so obvious. The program must be promoted not only in the community. An even more difficult selling job is often necessary with the faculty who, while they might vote for the program, are capable of giving it a crippling sort of half-hearted support. The complexities of the problem are well summed up in the following observations by the chairman of the committee on graduate study in one of the cooperating colleges:

> It seems to me that at least 75% of the faculty should possess the doctorate (75% of those teaching graduate courses). But more important, there must be 100% acceptance and enthusiasm for graduate work on the part of the total faculty and the administration.

Thus the initial planning must concern itself not only with setting up minimum acceptable standards for faculty and facilities but with what Dean DeVane of Yale University has alluded to as "a degree of low animal cunning."

Dean DeVane was referring, in this statement, to one of the essential qualities of a good academic dean. One of the essential qualities of a good graduate program, whether in a large university or a small college, is the quality of its academic leadership. If possible, the very first step in planning a new graduate program, therefore, should be to select the person who will lead it. Or perhaps even earlier, a careful definition of his authority and responsibility should be agreed upon by the faculty and administration. The failure to do this has resulted in the situation so vividly described by Roy F. Nichols in his article "The Ambiguous Position of the Graduate-School Dean." [3] One of the respondents, in fact, suggested that the director of the program should be chosen long before any faculty vote is taken and that he should spend his first year making clear to both faculty and administration the specific provisions which are necessary for the program to be effective.

Two other caveats relating to the administration of graduate programs appear in a variety of the questionnaires. First, the graduate school should, ideally, be totally independent from undergraduate control. This does not preclude the responsibility's residing in the officer who has charge of the over-all academic interests of the institution; but he must have the capacity and the right to wear a separate hat as the occasion demands. And second, the relationships among the departments offering graduate study and between the department heads and the director of the program must be precisely defined. Anything short of complete understanding concerning the areas of authority among these officers cannot but handicap severely either an infant or a mature graduate program. Even where graduate work is offered in one department only, there is a strong argument in favor of assigning the responsibility of direct supervision to an academic officer with wider authority than that generally accorded a departmental chairman.

A second administrative consideration which demands both immediate and continued attention is the financing of the graduate program. Because of the casual approach which seems to characterize many of the colleges in this study, and despite the argument that the size of their programs favors this approach, it is desirable for the di-

---

3. *Journal of Higher Education* XXX (March, 1959), pp. 123-27. See also Oliver C. Carmichael, *Graduate Education: A Critique and a Program* (New York: Harper & Brothers, 1961), pp. 188-94.

rector, working with the financial officer of the college, to make a careful cost analysis preliminary to undertaking graduate study. It is even more important that it be done periodically in order that the college may be able to gauge the extent of its graduate commitment. For if the case presented in Sidney G. Tickton's *Needed: A Ten Year College Budget*[4] is sound—and his case is hard to refute—then a vast majority of the privately supported colleges will be confronted in the very near future with financial problems much more severe than the ones they have learned to live with in the past. The cost of running a graduate program of real quality may be far more than the college can rightly sustain if it is to meet its more basic undergraduate commitments. But because of the many attractive benefits accruing from such a program, there is temptation to undertake too much with too little and to spread the financial resources of the institution dangerously thin. Several of the colleges, of course, have received financial support from foundations. Hopefully, other foundations or agencies will come to see the desirability of encouraging comparable developments in deserving colleges. To date, however, such support has tended to be diverted to the larger and more prestigious institutions. Why, for example, should not the NDEA fellowships be more generally available for the graduate student in the small colleges?

In the meantime, unless the college is prepared to finance the graduate program for a period of at least three to five years, and has the resources to afford such a development, it should resist all blandishments in this area. As one respondent has written: "I know of few private liberal arts colleges with adequate financial resources—adequate to the needs of the undergraduate program. Unless a college has such resources, plus the additional resources necessary in an era of almost certain inflation, my suggestion is: stick to your knitting." The writer might well have suggested that tuition for the graduate student be increased over that charged the undergraduate, representing some realistic apportionment of the costs of instruction. For the graduate program must be paid for in some way, and the alternatives are not necessarily desirable. For example, undergraduate sections may have to be substantially enlarged; faculty teaching loads may, perforce, be held at too high a level; graduate scholarships may be paid for out of the already limited resources for undergraduate student aid; an undue

4.   New York: The Fund for the Advancement of Education, 1961.

portion of the income from endowment or gifts may be diverted to graduate costs; graduate or teaching assistants of marginal ability may be employed to relieve faculty for graduate instruction.

On this last point, the director of a long-established graduate program writes:

> It seems to be impractical to offer graduate courses and a master's program for graduate teaching assistants if the number of assistants is less than four in one department, because more staff time will be required to put on the program than the teaching help secured from the assistants. A liberal arts college with strong undergraduate majors can, however, admit as graduate students good candidates from institutions with less strong undergraduate majors. These candidates can strengthen their undergraduate training by completing the stronger major, by taking one or two real graduate courses, and by completing a demanding research thesis. The liberal arts college profits by the presence of such candidates, and the candidates, after receiving the master's degree, are ready for the stiff competition of the big graduate school. We believe that we make a real contribution to the education of such candidates.

But contribution or no contribution, there is in this passage a warning to the institution that thinks it can develop its graduate program largely on the possibility of finding low-cost relief for its undergraduate instructional budget.

A word of caution, too, should be given to the colleges which are under pressure from one or more local industries to provide graduate instruction for their employees. Unless the sponsors are willing to make a real investment, the college should walk warily. If the work is given in industrial facilities, the college receives no benefit in the form of additions to its own educational resources. If the program is partially subsidized through the addition of dollar-a-year instructors, the college should make certain that this represents a long-range commitment and, further, that it has some control over the time that the instructor is free to devote to his academic responsibilities. For the common experience, after the initial glow has waned somewhat, is that both the contributing organization and the participating individual tend to lose some of their enthusiasm.

In the whole area of financial administration, there are compelling grounds for favoring separate budgeting for graduate instruction. Whether or not the graduate program carries a proportional share of the total operating overhead, the administration has an obligation to make a realistic assessment of the cost of this commitment. For the colleges in the group included in this study are essentially undergraduate colleges and, as privately supported institutions, relatively few of them have resources comparable with those of the larger private or the tax-supported universities. It follows that these resources must be carefully husbanded.

At the risk of overemphasizing the financial considerations, it might be useful to look at the budgetary implications of graduate study as related to facilities, students, and faculty. This is not to say that these three areas should be viewed only from the financial standpoint, but merely that this is obviously a focal consideration.

A weakness of many of the graduate programs in the independently structured colleges is that there has simply been no investment for the graduate student in the way of special facilities to enhance his educational experience. It is one thing to increase the library holdings in areas of graduate instruction, but unless some carrels or other study facilities are provided, the graduate student—even the full-time graduate student—will miss the impetus to personal study and research which such accommodations provide. As for the part-time students, they require something more than mere opportunity to ensure that they utilize the library. Many of them need to be not so much led as driven if they are to go beyond the mere textbook in their graduate preparation. Therefore, ideally the library should have a special room set aside for such graduate programs as those in education so that the busy teacher-student may, with relative ease and dispatch, have access to the primary and secondary materials necessary for the efficacy of his educational endeavors.

Moreover, as is evident in the chapter on finance and facilities, very few of the colleges provide anything in the way of meeting places where graduate students may congregate for purposes of intellectual or social exchange. Separate dormitories are desirable for the full-time students. At the very least a graduate lounge is essential for the part-time students. And a genuine effort should be made both departmentally and school-wide to bring the graduate students together for periodic meetings with fellow students and faculty. If the small college does not provide at least some measure of opportunity for such interchange, it may well fail in its mission.

A graduate program of quality cannot be carried on by simply making undergraduate facilities available to the advanced student. More in the way of research materials, of visual aids, of laboratory space, and the like must be provided if the work is to be truly graduate, and not just an extension of undergraduate, study. And all of this costs money.

As for the students, the small graduate program is not, in any realistic sense, in competition with the large university. It cannot hope, under normal circumstances, to attract a high percentage of top-level students. Exceptions to this principle are to be found among the colleges included in this study; but these are the exceptions, not the rule. Thus, it is extremely important, in the initial stages, that the college make a careful examination of the potential supply of graduate students of quality. Moreover, this study must be repeated periodically. For a specialized program which enjoys an active demand at the outset may quickly consume the available supply of qualified enrollees. One college estimates that a minimum of six full-time and six part-time students is necessary in each area in which graduate study is given. Other institutions, however, with less in the way of financial support may find this number far below the minimal requirement.

In their desire to build up graduate programs, it is difficult for many colleges to resist accepting students whose academic potential is below standard. Even in programs which are populated largely by elementary or secondary school teachers, the tendency is to assume that the person, because he is teaching, is capable of profiting from graduate instruction. This attitude is challenged by the chairman of the graduate committee in one of the outstanding institutions in this survey: "I feel that liberal arts colleges need to recognize that many teachers are not prepared to undertake full-fledged master's work in a specific subject matter field." The writer goes on to say that these persons may well profit from some additional work in the liberal arts, suggesting that a specialized curriculum might be devised for them instead of the graduate courses in the field of education in which they are generally enrolled.

Another pertinent admonition comes from one of the faculty questionnaires: "Do not allow the desire to attract undergraduate laboratory assistants to eclipse the importance of having a first-rate graduate program; insist on able graduate students, not just anyone capable of correcting freshman papers." In other words, the temptation to get laboratory and tutorial assistants may well prove to be something of a Lorelei if it is not vigorously controlled.

On the other hand, many colleges can improve their instructional program by the use of graduate assistants and can provide a highly important experience for the students themselves through the close supervision of apprenticeship activities, which is feasible in the smaller setting. It is even possible, as was demonstrated in some of the colleges, to devise means whereby the graduate assistant comes in both social and intellectual contact with the undergraduate, thus providing the type of rapprochement which can improve the quality of learning on both levels and possibly induce in the graduate student a strong interest in entering the profession of college teaching. A similar effect can be achieved by developing a program of extracurricular activities for the graduate student, including the opportunity to hear outstanding teachers and scholars from other institutions. In a sense, much of this is peripheral to providing stimulation through a good counseling program in which the graduate student's needs are understood and his aspirations are encouraged. This may, in fact, be occurring, but there was evidence in this study that the counseling was for the most part conducted on an unorganized basis.

But all of this takes time; and in the academic world, as in many other walks of life, time is expensive. The college must determine whether it is willing to pay the price.

It is possible, as was suggested earlier, for the small college to uncover relatively untapped sources of high-quality graduate students who are not in the competitive market. One of these is local business and industry. Another, as discovered by a few colleges, is the neighboring housewife. In both these "professions" are many persons whose economic and intellectual well-being can be fostered through advanced study. But it need hardly be added that a selling job will have to be done to convince them that the personal expenditure of time, money, and effort is worthwhile. And again, this takes time, money, and effort on the part of the institution itself. Yet there are many such persons within commuting distance of almost every college who could make a real contribution through the type of advanced graduate training which the institution can provide. Particularly the college-trained housewives comprise a valuable source of potential college teachers who, though they will presumably not go on for the Ph.D., could be effective in the classroom if they received the level of training represented by the master's degree.

Even though the small college may not feel that it can make a large investment to recruit the topflight graduate student—and the hard reality is that such a student cannot be attracted to the small college in any numbers unless an investment is made—they must invest in their faculty if the program is to achieve distinction. It is an indisputable fact that graduate instruction of real merit requires not just more preparation on the part of the faculty than undergraduate instruction but also somewhat different qualifications, if not qualities. Nearly every major graduate school has on its staff professors who are as unsuccessful with undergraduates as they are successful with graduate students. Although the upgrading of undergraduate instruction in recent years may have lessened the gap somewhat, this will doubtless continue to be true. And the distinctive quality of these persons would appear to be their personal dedication to the search for truth through research. Therefore, the faculty members in the small college who are assigned graduate courses at least should have made a commitment to, if not achieved, some distinction in scholarship, a distinction directly related to their productivity in significant publication and research.

As was seen in many of the replies, a genuine effort must be made to ensure that the faculty members have time not only to prepare for their graduate courses but also to carry on the personal study which is so essential a concomitant of successful graduate instruction. They must not be overburdened. On the contrary, they should carry lighter loads than the members of the faculty involved solely in teaching undergraduates. Very often this means augmenting the faculty ranks. It also means relief from many of the clerical duties which accompany college teaching, with some of this relief preferably provided by graduate assistants. The practice of a number of colleges in having the graduate courses over and above the regular teaching load is scarcely defensible.

Moreover, these graduate instructors should be given every possible encouragement to attend professional meetings and to avail themselves of generous leaves of absence for purposes of personal advancement and stimulation. To avoid any letdown, they should experience the occasional competition of having a distinguished visiting professor from another campus serve as their colleague *pro tem*. And, as one of the respondents pointed out, "opportunity should be provided during the year for colloquies with colleagues in other institutions, or for that matter, with each other." "One of the advantages of maintaining a small graduate program," he continues, "is the facility with which its approach can be integrated and unified. But this is possible only if the staff can spend considerable time discussing common problems."

Another danger is that the graduate instructor may lose touch with the essential business of the institution, which is the teaching of undergraduates. Some of the larger universities, in order to avoid this danger, insist that even their senior graduate professors do a periodic stint in the undergraduate classroom or laboratory. The small college, of course, usually avoids this since, as was noted in Chapter IV, the usual practice calls for a teaching load which combines both graduate and undergraduate instruction.

One final note here: the faculty members assigned to graduate courses should, for the most part, have attained the doctorate. Whereas possession of the degree by no means guarantees that the individual is equipped to conduct graduate instruction of quality, it indicates a level of accomplishment that presupposes a philosophical, even psychological, grasp of the distinctive quality of graduate instruction.

And again the admonition, all of this costs money. The college that is unwilling or unable to make this investment should neither enter nor continue a graduate program. For, as one of the deans states the case, "A small graduate program must be as excellent as possible. There is in it almost no margin for error, for its few M.A.'s must be of indisputable quality."

In view of the earlier injunction calling for each college to make a study of the particular demand in terms of its available resources and to devise its program within that particular frame of reference, it may seem inconsistent to offer suggestions about standards, programs, and curriculums; and yet there are enough common denominators to justify generalized discussion here.

Without exception the administrators and faculty members consulted during the campus visits emphasized the importance of standards, indicating concern with standards in their own programs as well as with the standards of the master's degree in general. Accordingly, the preceding discussion contained many references to factors which militate against the maintenance of exacting requirements; but unless the small college succeeds in overcoming these handicaps, it can do little but contribute to the general debasement of the degree. While recognizing that the likelihood of many winners of Woodrow Wilson National Fellowships enrolling in the smaller college is not great—except in those few institutions which have achieved unusual prestige through their undergraduate programs—the liberal arts college must certainly avoid the opposite extreme of accepting any casual "shopper" who may wish to register for graduate courses. Further, in accordance with the practice of many of the larger graduate schools, some of the respondents recommended that a sharp distinction be made, after 15 to 18 hours, between candidates for degrees and the graduate students with more limited objectives.

The replies from a few of the institutions, in fact, suggest that standards for admission to graduate study are less selective than those for admission to the undergraduate freshman class. If this is true, it is a rather sad commentary on the quality of the graduate program. Particularly since the colleges do not have what has been referred to as "automatic prestige," there would certainly seem to be a special need for setting realistic, but nonetheless demanding, requirements for both admission and progression toward the degree. One of the faculty members expresses the problem as follows:

> We need to make the procedures and philosophy of the graduate degree more explicit and less informal. More standardization of comprehensive examination and final oral procedures is needed so that there is not so much variance in treatment of students. We need to be more careful in selecting graduate students and also to do some weeding out before they get to the stage where we practically have to give them the degree because they have been around so long.

At least one of the respondents called for a moderate point of view, pointing out that the master's degree is not, after all, the same as the doctorate and urging that the college, in its effort to ensure quality of performance, not be misled into thinking that a high attrition rate is necessarily a sign of a high-level program. In general, though, the replies suggest that the danger lies at the other end of the scale. This makes it especially important to establish checkpoints along the way. Thus one of the colleges offers the following advice:

> Give the candidate a stiff preliminary written and oral examination before he is allowed to proceed to the writing of the thesis, and make final examinations more or less a defense of the thesis. This ensures that the candidate has time to strengthen weak places in his preparation, or else makes it possible to drop him before he has invested time and energy in the thesis, after which all concerned feel under some pressure to grant the degree.[5]

5. See also R. E. Dunbar and J. W. Broberg, "Graduate Examination Practices

In this matter of standards much thought must be given to the place of the thesis in the master's degree regimen. The authors join many other writers on the subject of graduate study in the hope that the thesis, in some form, will be retained. A very appealing case is made by Dr. Carmichael, in his book *Graduate Education,* for a thesis which involves research on one or more "central concepts." [6] The specific topics which he suggests are certainly within the grasp of the average candidate for the degree. The master's exercise should provide an opportunity for experience with conducting research, with effective presentation, and with an investigation which has either depth or breadth or both, but which is not necessarily "original" to the extent ordinarily required for the doctoral dissertation.

In many of the replies emphasis is placed on the necessity of arriving at a consistent and clear definition of the limits of the master's thesis. On this level, as well as on the doctoral level, there is too much individual variation in the demands of different thesis supervisors. Thus, here is an area where agreement on the part of the faculty should be achieved so as to ensure relative consistency of expectation.

Moreover, the master's programs in the small colleges should place emphasis upon term papers and other written work, regardless of the level of research they may represent, in every course where such an exercise is relevant. Without in any way underemphasizing the importance of fluency in a foreign language, it is recommended that a high level of competence be demanded in the use of the English language as a medium of written expression. The liberal arts college would seem to be in a particularly advantageous position to insist upon such a requirement.

As for methodology in the classroom, very few replies were hostile to the idea of commingling advanced undergraduates with graduate students, or to the use of the lecture method which this practice generally makes necessary. On the other hand, at least ten of the questionnaires called for more seminar-type courses limited strictly to graduate students. Since the seminar has become almost the traditional vehicle for graduate instruction of high calibre, it would certainly seem incumbent upon the liberal arts college to provide opportunity

---

at the M.S. and M.A. Levels," *Journal of Chemical Education* XXXVII (May, 1960), p. 254.
6.   Carmichael, *op. cit.,* p. 125.

for seminars that are truly graduate seminars, not just small discussion groups. Even the mention here seems like stressing the obvious; and yet the statistical data in Chapter VI suggest the need for this recommendation. Moreover, the replies from some of the graduate students indicate that the programs in their schools are deficient in the amount of independent study which they permit or encourage. Since the graduate seminar places major responsibility upon the participants, its presence is essential in a good graduate program. Another suggestion is to provide seminars with more than one faculty member in charge, as well as seminars cutting across disciplines. The over-all objectives of the graduate program, of course, would play a role in the decision to institute this type of course.

This last point raises the question of the type of graduate program which the small college should undertake; and here again the answer must come from the school itself, consistent with its own estimate of needs and capabilities. Nevertheless, it might be interesting to record here some of the thoughtful observations which appeared in many of the replies.

First and foremost, from every side came the strong insistence that the college should have a graduate *program*, rather than a mere schedule of courses. There seems to be a haunting fear, doubtless born of reality, that a fragmented, shopping-center offering will be developed in lieu of the type of curriculum which makes possible a comprehensive view of an organized field. Similarly, many of the replies emphasized the necessity of providing graduate programs in more than one department, even at the risk of overextension. Preferably, of course, the departments should be closely related so that they will naturally support each other's programs. This will avoid what is seen as a danger in some colleges, which is building a graduate program around one or two outstanding professors. It makes possible also the development of interdepartmental and interdivisional degrees supported by the pooled resources of more than one area. In such ways as this, it is suggested, the student can enjoy an experience different from that generally available in the larger university, where a high degree of specialization is the order of the day.

Over and over again replies emphasized the necessity of developing distinctive strengths in the graduate program. As was seen in Chapter VI, many of the colleges have done just that. The curriculum might be designed for the training of teachers for junior, or even senior, colleges. As this report urged earlier, the development of such programs may indeed be a matter of basic survival for many of the smaller colleges, as competition for faculty members continues to increase. It may be some modification of the Carmichael Master of Philosophy degree.[7] Through the quality of supervision which it can provide, the small college can afford its graduate students an invaluable experience as apprentice teachers. To the argument that this will protract the time required for the degree, one can only point to no less an authority than Dean Elder of the Graduate School at Harvard, who discovered that providing teaching experience for the doctoral candidates at Harvard and Radcliffe added only a half year to the average time required for completing the Ph.D. degree.

The distinctive curriculum could be a modification of the Master of Arts in Teaching. Here again, as many thoughtful persons have pointed out, the liberal arts college is in a particularly effective position to make a contribution. One desirable feature in the development of the M.A.T. program is that it can be treated as a terminal degree, since presumably only a limited number of the recipients will go on for a doctorate. Therefore, more experimentation and individual variation is feasible. One possible danger in this area, however, is a tendency toward the professionalization of the degree; in other words, toward greater emphasis in the course content and methodology upon the "how" as distinct from the "why."

Whatever approach the liberal arts college takes in its master's programs, many of the persons with whom this subject was discussed emphasized that the program must be appropriate to the institution offering it. Thus, one of the faculty respondents wrote:

> There has to be some special reason for creating an M.A. program— unique facilities, outstanding relationships for work-study opportunities with supporting agencies in the community (clinics, industry, hospitals, research organization, etc.), particularly competent or productive faculty, and so forth. In this way, students will come to apply for admission not because the college is nearby but because it offers features not to be found in a university setting. If the programs are mere copies of the university, little is to be gained.

In repeating this statement, however, there is no intention to discourage the college from seeking ways of cooperating with other com-

7. *Loc. cit.*

parable colleges or with nearby universities. Some years ago the suggestion was made by Frank Bowles of the College Entrance Examination Board that the major universities should serve as hubs in an academic wheel, with the spokes going out to the smaller campuses. A somewhat similar suggestion was made by Dr. Carmichael in his recent evaluation of graduate study when he proposed having the small college start graduate work by using something comparable with the Commonwealth (English-speaking) system of affiliating new programs with established universities. The cooperative approach may indeed be one way to encourage an expansion of graduate opportunities while at the same time ensuring a reasonable consistency in level of performance.

Nevertheless, it has been one of the premises of this study that the private liberal arts college, in part because of its size, is in a position to bring back to the master's degree some of the vitality which it once possessed, as well as something of its original meaning, which called for the student's becoming a "master" in his field. Great is the need and great is the potential gain from an approach combining courage and creative vigor in the development of programs of distinctive merit. Some of these already exist on individual campuses. A few exist through the efforts of several colleges working together.

One need of our country is a substantial increase in graduate opportunities. An even greater need is for an improved quality in graduate instruction, particularly on the master's level. There can be no doubt that here is an area where the independent liberal arts college can, by taking thought, add cubits to its stature and, at the same time, be of enlarged usefulness to the community it serves.

APPENDIX I

Colleges in the Study

1. Abilene Christian College, Abilene, Texas
2. Albion College, Albion, Michigan
3. Alfred University, Alfred, New York
4. Allegheny College, Meadville, Pennsylvania
5. American International College, Springfield, Massachusetts
6. Amherst College, Amherst, Massachusetts
7. Antioch College, Yellow Springs, Ohio
8. Aquinas College, Grand Rapids, Michigan
9. Assumption College, Worcester, Massachusetts
10. Athenaeum of Ohio, The, Cincinnati, Ohio
11. Austin College, Sherman, Texas
12. Barry College, Miami, Florida
13. Beloit College, Beloit, Wisconsin
14. Bennington College, Bennington, Vermont
15. Birmingham-Southern College, Birmingham, Alabama
16. Bucknell University, Lewisburg, Pennsylvania
17. California Western University, San Diego, California
18. Canisius College, Buffalo, New York
19. Cardinal Stritch College, Milwaukee, Wisconsin
20. Colgate University, Hamilton, New York
21. College Misericordia, Dallas, Pennsylvania
22. College of Idaho, Caldwell, Idaho
23. College of Our Lady of the Elms, Chicopee, Massachusetts
24. College of St. Rose, The, Albany, New York
25. College of St. Thomas, St. Paul, Minnesota
26. College of the Holy Cross, Worcester, Massachusetts
27. College of the Holy Names, Oakland, California
28. College of the Pacific, Stockton, California (name changed to University of the Pacific in 1961)
29. Colorado College, Colorado Springs, Colorado
30. Connecticut College, New London, Connecticut
31. DePauw University, Greencastle, Indiana
32. Dominican College of San Rafael, San Rafael, California
33. Drury College, Springfield, Missouri
34. Earlham College, Richmond, Indiana
35. Elmira College, Elmira, New York
36. Emmanuel Missionary College, Berrien Springs, Michigan (name changed to Andrews University in 1961)

143

37. Fairfield University, Fairfield, Connecticut
38. Fisk University, Nashville, Tennessee
39. Franklin and Marshall College, Lancaster, Pennsylvania
40. Furman University, Greenville, South Carolina
41. Gallaudet College, Washington, D. C.
42. George Williams College, Chicago, Illinois
43. Georgetown College, Georgetown, Kentucky
44. Gonzaga University, Spokane, Washington
45. Goucher College, Baltimore, Maryland
46. Guilford College, Guilford College, North Carolina
47. Hampton Institute, Hampton, Virginia
48. Hardin-Simmons University, Abilene, Texas
49. Harding College, Searcy, Arkansas
50. Haverford College, Haverford, Pennsylvania
51. Hobart and William Smith Colleges, Geneva, New York
52. Hollins College, Hollins, Virginia
53. Howard Payne College, Brownwood, Texas
54. Illinois Wesleyan University, Bloomington, Illinois
55. Immaculate Heart College, Los Angeles, California
56. Incarnate Word College, San Antonio, Texas
57. Ithaca College, Ithaca, New York
58. La Sierra College, Arlington, California
59. Lewis and Clark College, Portland, Oregon
60. Linfield College, McMinnville, Oregon
61. Loyola College, Baltimore, Maryland
62. Loyola University of Los Angeles, Los Angeles, California
63. Macalester College, St. Paul, Minnesota
64. MacMurray College, Jacksonville, Illinois
65. Manhattanville College of the Sacred Heart, Purchase, New York
66. Marywood College, Scranton, Pennsylvania
67. McMurry College, Abilene, Texas
68. Mercer University, Macon, Georgia
69. Middlebury College, Middlebury, Vermont
70. Midwestern University, Wichita Falls, Texas
71. Millikin University, Decatur, Illinois
72. Mills College, Oakland, California
73. Mississippi College, Clinton, Mississippi
74. Mount Holyoke College, South Hadley, Massachusetts
75. Mount St. Mary College, Hooksett, New Hampshire
76. Mount St. Mary's College, Los Angeles, California
77. Nazareth College, Louisville, Kentucky
78. Nazareth College, Rochester, New York
79. Niagara University, Niagara Falls, New York
80. Oberlin College, Oberlin, Ohio
81. Ohio Wesleyan University, Delaware, Ohio
82. Pacific Lutheran University, Tacoma, Washington
83. Pacific Union College, Angwin, California
84. Pasadena College, Pasadena, California
85. Pepperdine College, Los Angeles, California
86. Phillips University, Enid, Oklahoma

87. Providence College, Providence, Rhode Island
88. Reed College, Portland, Oregon
89. Rivier College, Nashua, New Hampshire
90. Rockford College, Rockford, Illinois
91. Rollins College, Winter Park, Florida
92. Rosary College, River Forest, Illinois
93. Russell Sage College, Troy, New York
94. St. Bernardine of Siena College, Loudonville, New York
95. St. Francis College, Fort Wayne, Indiana
96. St. John's College, Annapolis, Maryland
97. St. Joseph College, West Hartford, Connecticut
98. St. Lawrence University, Canton, New York
99. St. Mary College, Xavier, Kansas
100. St. Mary's College, Winona, Minnesota
101. St. Mary's College of California, St. Mary's College P.O., California
102. St. Mary's University of San Antonio, San Antonio, Texas
103. St. Michael's College, Winooski, Vermont
104. St. Vincent College, Latrobe, Pennsylvania
105. St. Xavier College, Chicago, Illinois
106. San Diego College for Women, San Diego, California
107. San Francisco College for Women, San Francisco, California
108. Sarah Lawrence College, Bronxville, New York
109. Seattle University, Seattle, Washington
110. Siena Heights College, Adrian, Michigan
111. Simmons College, Boston, Massachusetts
112. Smith College, Northampton, Massachusetts
113. Springfield College, Springfield, Massachusetts
114. Stetson University, De Land, Florida
115. Suffolk University, Boston, Massachusetts
116. Swarthmore College, Swarthmore, Pennsylvania
117. Texas Wesleyan College, Fort Worth, Texas
118. Trinity College, Hartford, Connecticut
119. Trinity University, San Antonio, Texas
120. Tuskegee Institute, Tuskegee, Alabama
121. Union College, Barbourville, Kentucky
122. Union College, Schenectady, New York
123. University of Chattanooga, Chattanooga, Tennessee
124. University of Puget Sound, Tacoma, Washington
125. University of Redlands, Redlands, California
126. University of Scranton, Scranton, Pennsylvania
127. University of the South, Sewanee, Tennessee
128. Vassar College, Poughkeepsie, New York
129. Wagner College, Staten Island, New York
130. Walla Walla College, College Place, Washington
131. Wellesley College, Wellesley, Massachusetts
132. Wells College, Aurora, New York
133. Wesleyan University, Middletown, Connecticut
134. Western Maryland College, Westminster, Maryland
135. Westminster College, New Wilmington, Pennsylvania
136. Wheaton College, Wheaton, Illinois

137. Whittier College, Whittier, California
138. Whitworth College, Spokane, Washington
139. Wilkes College, Wilkes-Barre, Pennsylvania
140. Willamette University, Salem, Oregon
141. Williams College, Williamstown, Massachusetts
142. Wittenberg University, Springfield, Ohio
143. Xavier University, New Orleans, Louisiana

Colleges Visited

1. Abilene Christian College, Abilene, Texas
2. Allegheny College, Meadville, Pennsylvania
3. Amherst College, Amherst, Massachusetts
4. Birmingham-Southern College, Birmingham, Alabama
5. Bucknell University, Lewisburg, Pennsylvania
6. California Western University, San Diego, California
7. Colgate University, Hamilton, New York
8. College Misericordia, Dallas, Pennsylvania
9. DePauw University, Greencastle, Indiana
10. Drury College, Springfield, Missouri
11. Earlham College, Richmond, Indiana
12. Elmira College, Elmira, New York
13. Franklin and Marshall College, Lancaster, Pennsylvania
14. Furman University, Greenville, South Carolina
15. Goucher College, Baltimore, Maryland
16. Hardin-Simmons University, Abilene, Texas
17. Haverford College, Haverford, Pennsylvania
18. Hollins College, Hollins, Virginia
19. MacMurray College, Jacksonville, Illinois
20. Marywood College, Scranton, Pennsylvania
21. McMurry College, Abilene, Texas
22. Mercer University, Macon, Georgia
23. Nazareth College, Rochester, New York
24. Oberlin College, Oberlin, Ohio
25. Ohio Wesleyan University, Delaware, Ohio
26. Pepperdine College, Los Angeles, California
27. Phillips University, Enid, Oklahoma
28. Rollins College, Winter Park, Florida
29. St. Vincent College, Latrobe, Pennsylvania
30. Sarah Lawrence College, Bronxville, New York
31. Smith College, Northampton, Massachusetts
32. Stetson University, De Land, Florida
33. Swarthmore College, Swarthmore, Pennsylvania
34. Trinity College, Hartford, Connecticut
35. University of Redlands, Redlands, California
36. University of Scranton, Scranton, Pennsylvania
37. Vassar College, Poughkeepsie, New York
38. Wesleyan University, Middletown, Connecticut

39. Western Maryland College, Westminster, Maryland
40. Westminster College, New Wilmington, Pennsylvania
41. Wilkes Colleges, Wilkes-Barre, Pennsylvania
42. Williams College, Williamstown, Massachusetts

Colleges Cooperating in Sample
of Graduate Faculty and Students

1. Abilene Christian College, Abilene, Texas
2. Allegheny College, Meadville, Pennsylvania
3. Austin College, Sherman, Texas
4. Birmingham-Southern College, Birmingham, Alabama
5. California Western University, San Diego, California
6. Colgate University, Hamilton, New York
7. College of Idaho, Caldwell, Idaho
8. College of the Holy Names, Oakland, California
9. Connecticut College, New London, Connecticut
10. Dominican College of San Rafael, San Rafael, California
11. Drury College, Springfield, Missouri
12. Emmanuel Missionary College, Berrien Springs, Michigan
13. Furman University, Greenville, South Carolina
14. Gonzaga University, Spokane, Washington
15. Hardin-Simmons University, Abilene, Texas
16. Hollins College, Hollins, Virginia
17. Incarnate Word College, San Antonio, Texas
18. Loyola College, Baltimore, Maryland
19. Macalester College, St. Paul, Minnesota
20. Manhattanville College of the Sacred Heart, Purchase, New York
21. Marywood College, Scranton, Pennsylvania
22. Mercer University, Macon, Georgia
23. Mills College, Oakland, California
24. Mount Holyoke College, South Hadley, Massachusetts
25. Nazareth College, Louisville, Kentucky
26. Ohio Wesleyan University, Delaware, Ohio
27. Pepperdine College, Los Angeles, California
28. Rivier College, Nashua, New Hampshire
29. Rollins College, Winter Park, Florida
30. Russell Sage College, Troy, New York
31. St. Francis College, Fort Wayne, Indiana
32. St. Lawrence University, Canton, New York
33. St. Mary's College, Winona, Minnesota
34. St. Xavier College, Chicago, Illinois
35. San Francisco College for Women, San Francisco, California
36. Seattle University, Seattle, Washington
37. Simmons College, Boston, Massachusetts
38. Stetson University, De Land, Florida
39. Swarthmore College, Swarthmore, Pennsylvania

40. Trinity College, Hartford, Connecticut
41. Trinity University, San Antonio, Texas
42. Union College, Schenectady, New York
43. University of Redlands, Redlands, California
44. Wellesley College, Wellesley, Massachusetts
45. Western Maryland College, Westminster, Maryland
46. Wheaton College, Wheaton, Illinois
47. Whitworth College, Spokane, Washington
48. Williams College, Williamstown, Massachusetts
49. Wittenberg University, Springfield, Ohio
50. Xavier University, New Orleans, Louisiana

APPENDIX II

Questionnaires

Questionnaire "A": *To All Private Institutions with Enrollment under 2,500*

1. Are you basically an undergraduate liberal arts institution?

   Yes...... No...... Enrollment..........

2. If yes,

   A. Do you offer the doctorate? Yes...... No......
   B. Do you offer the Master of Arts and/or Science degree?

   Yes...... No......

   C. (1) If you do not now offer the master's program, have you done so in the past 10 years? Yes...... No......

   (2) If not now, are you planning a master's program?

   Yes...... No......

3. With whom can we communicate concerning your experience with, or plans for, the master's program?

   ....
   Name and Title

   ....
   Name of Institution

Questionnaire "B": *To All Colleges in Category*

BLUEPRINTS FOR GRADUATE STUDY

Institution ....

Name ....

College Position ....

Title in Relation to Graduate Program ....

I. HISTORY AND PURPOSE

A. In what academic year did you offer your first graduate instruction?.......

B. Why and how was your graduate program initiated?

    1. Did you use the services of a consultant? Yes...... No......

    2. In what department or departments was graduate study first offered?

C. How did you evaluate the capacity of your college for offering graduate study?

D. What authorization or approval was necessary to undertake the offering of your graduate program? (i.e., charter revision, trustee action, regional association, state requirements, etc.)

E. During the first year of your graduate program how many of your students were drawn from:

    1. Your own undergraduate college........

    2. Your own state........

    3. Your church constituency........

    4. Your immediate locality........

    5. Nearby colleges........

    6. Other........

II. PRESENT CHARACTERISTICS OF YOUR GRADUATE PROGRAM

A. *Administration:*

    1. Which administrator(s) or group has the immediate responsibility for the following areas:

        a. Admission of students.......................................

        b. Curriculum...

        c. General examinations.......................................

        d. Schedules...

        e. Records..

        f. Budget...

        g. Classroom assignments.....................................

        h. Counseling...

        i. Social activity..

        j. Placement service..

B. *Faculty (1959-60):*

    1. How many members of your graduate faculty teach:

        a. Graduate courses only........

        b. Both graduate and undergraduate courses........

        c. Full time........

150

d. Part time........

     (1) Source of part time faculty members.

2. Is graduate instruction considered part of, or over and above, the normal teaching load?

3. How do the qualifications for your graduate faculty differ from those for your undergraduate faculty?

4. Is there a difference in teaching load between graduate and undergraduate faculty members?

5. Is there a difference in compensation between graduate and undergraduate faculty members?

6. What provisions are made to encourage graduate faculty members to do research?

C. *Students:*

  1. Enrollment:

    a. Total graduate enrollment 1960........1955........1950........

      1. Full time 1960........

      2. Part time 1960........

      3. Summer only 1960........

      4. Academic year 1960........

      5. Graduate students housed in resident facilities or within the immediate vicinity of the campus 1960........

      6. Men enrolled 1960........

      7. Teachers (K-12) enrolled 1960........

      8. Number of students enrolled from your undergraduate program of 1960........

    b. Master's degrees awarded 1960........1955........1950........

      1. Master of arts degrees awarded 1960........

      2. Master of science degrees awarded 1960........

  2. Do any of your graduate students teach undergraduate courses?

    Yes...... No...... If yes, how many?........

  3. What other services (for compensation) do your graduate students perform for the college?

  4. What percentage of your graduate courses contain undergraduate students?........

    a. What percentage of graduate courses are limited to graduate students?........

  5. What percentage of your graduate students on completion of the master's degree in 1959-60:

    a. Are continuing work to the doctorate........

b. Are taking positions in industry........

c. Are teaching in college........

d. Are teaching in school (K-12)........

e. Other........

D. *Finances and Facilities:*

1. What are the provisions made for financing your graduate program?

2. Was it necessary to add facilities to accommodate your graduate program? Yes...... No...... If yes, please explain.

3. What additional facilities would be helpful in the further development of your graduate program?

4. In what ways are you utilizing the resources of nearby institutions, industry, other?

E. *Curriculum:*

1. Does your graduate program contain any unique features?

F. *Evaluation:*

1. What do you consider the principal benefits derived from your graduate program?

2. What do you consider its chief disadvantages?

3. What general advice would you give a similar institution contemplating the inauguration of a graduate program?

Questionnaire "C": *To Graduate Faculty in Sample*

To assist us in making an analysis and evaluation of graduate study in small, privately controlled colleges and universities, we would appreciate your giving us the benefit of your ideas and experience by providing brief answers to the following questions. Neither you nor your institution will be identified in the use of any of the answers you provide.

This study is being conducted under the sponsorship of the Association of American Colleges with the aid of a grant from the Lilly Endowment.

1. On the basis of your present experience, what do you consider to be the particular advantages of maintaining a graduate program in a small, private, liberal arts college?

2. The disadvantages?

3. What personal benefits do you feel derive from your participation in the graduate program?

4. What personal disadvantages, if any?

5. What additional resources would be helpful in the further development of the graduate program at your college?

6. What suggestions could you make for the improvement of the Master's degree?

7. What suggestions would you offer another similar institution contemplating the inauguration of a Master's program?

Questionnaire "D": *To Graduate Students in Sample*

To assist us in making an analysis and evaluation of graduate study in small, privately controlled colleges and universities, we would appreciate your giving us the benefit of your ideas and experience by providing brief answers to the following questions. Neither you nor your institution will be identified in the use of any of the answers you provide.

1. What is your major field of graduate study?.............................
2. Are you engaged full time in graduate study? If not, what is your principal occupation?
3. Why have you enrolled for graduate study at this institution rather than a large university?
4. Do you plan graduate study beyond the M.A.? If so, what (Ph.D., Ed.D.,

   Certificate, other) ....

   why..

   where..

   when ....
5. How are you financing your graduate study?
6. What do you consider the particular strengths of your present graduate school?
7. Its particular weaknesses?
8. What suggestions could you offer for strengthening the requirements for the Master's degree?
9. Other comments.

Questionnaire "E": *Supplementary Questionnaire to All Colleges in Category*

I. *Curriculum*

A. Does your graduate program restrict the student to the area of his specialization, or is he permitted (or required) to elect courses from other fields? Please explain.

B. Do your graduate programs call for particular sequences of courses, or does the student elect courses as they are available and in the order he may choose? Please explain.

C. In your M.A. program for teachers, how many non-education courses does the candidate elect and apply toward his degree requirements? (1) Are these graduate courses or can they be courses on the undergraduate level? (2) What prerequisites, if any, does he need for these courses?

D. What percentage (estimated) of the normal graduate student's credits for the degree are or can be earned in

1. lecture or lecture-discussion courses........

2. seminars (exclusive of thesis seminars)........

3. thesis seminars........

4. the thesis itself........

5. independent study (exclusive of the thesis)........

6. research (exclusive of the thesis) ....

E. Please estimate the average length of time required by your candidates to complete their M.A. degree.

F. Please describe any features of your graduate curriculum which you consider particularly effective and/or unique. (Use additional space on the back, if needed.)

(This sheet may be detached and filled out by another officer if appropriate.)

II. *Finances and Facilities*

A. Is your graduate program budgeted separately?

B. Does it carry the same percentage of the institution's overhead as the undergraduate program? Please explain.

C. Does the graduate program "pay for itself"? Please estimate to what extent, if any, it is subsidized

1. by the undergraduate program........

2. by tuition paid by the graduate students........

3. by outside subsidy........
(Please explain the nature of the outside subsidy, if any.)

D. If your program began since World War II,

1. To what extent was your library budget increased to meet the needs of the graduate program?

2. What facilities were added exclusively or largely to meet the needs of the graduate program?

3. Are any of your present facilities used exclusively for your graduate students, faculty, instructors, or research? Please explain.

Nationally Recognized Accrediting Agencies
and Associations

(Published by the United States Commissioner of Education)

Accrediting Association of Bible Colleges
Accrediting Commission for Business Schools
American Association of Collegiate Schools of Business
American Association of Nurse Anesthetists
American Association of Schools of Religious Education
American Association of Theological Schools
American Bar Association
American Council on Education for Journalism
American Council on Pharmaceutical Education
American Osteopathic Association
American Podiatry Association
American Public Health Association
Commission on Accreditation of the Council on Social Work Education
Committee on Accreditation, American Library Association
Committee on Professional Training of the American Chemical Society
Council on Dental Education of the American Dental Association
Council on Education of the American Veterinary Medical Association
Council on Optometric Education of the American Optometric Association
Engineers' Council for Professional Development
Liaison Committee on Medical Education (Council on Medical Education and
  Hospitals of the American Medical Association and the Executive Council of
  the Association of American Medical Colleges)
Middle States Association of Colleges and Secondary Schools
National Architectural Accrediting Board
National Association of Schools of Music
National Council for Accreditation of Teacher Education
National League for Nursing, Inc.
New England Association of Colleges and Secondary Schools
New York Board of Regents (for higher institutions within New York State)
North Central Association of Colleges and Secondary Schools
Northwest Association of Secondary and Higher Schools
Society of American Foresters
Southern Association of Colleges and Schools
Western College Association (after July 1, 1962, Western Association of Schools
  and Colleges)

Accrediting Agencies and Associations
Recognized by the National Commission on Accrediting

REGIONAL ACCREDITING ASSOCIATIONS

Middle States Association of Colleges and Secondary Schools
New England Association of Colleges and Secondary Schools
North Central Association of Colleges and Secondary Schools
Northwest Association of Secondary and Higher Schools
Southern Association of Colleges and Schools
Western College Association (after July 1, 1962, Western Association of Schools and Colleges)

PROFESSIONAL ASSOCIATIONS

American Association of Collegiate Schools of Business
American Association of Theological Schools
American Bar Association
American Chemical Society
American Council on Education for Journalism
American Council on Pharmaceutical Education
American Dental Association
American Library Association
American Optometric Association
American Psychological Association
American Public Health Association
American Society of Landscape Architects
American Veterinary Medical Association
Association of American Law Schools
Council on Social Work Education
Engineers' Council for Professional Development
Liaison Committee on Medical Education
National Architectural Accrediting Board
National Association of Schools of Art
National Association of Schools of Music
National Council for Accreditation of Teacher Education
National League for Nursing, Inc.
Society of American Foresters

APPENDIX IV

Regional Guidelines

Several of the regional associations have provided materials for the use either of the institution in evaluating its potential for graduate study or of the association representatives in accreditation surveys. Since this material could be of use to any college now conducting, or considering, graduate study, portions are reproduced here, with the permission of the appropriate officers of the regional association. While the material is not limited to the master's level, it is nevertheless applicable.

Middle States Association of Colleges and Secondary Schools

"Graduate Work"

FACTORS WHICH AFFECT THE QUALITY OF GRADUATE WORK

1. *The clarity of its objectives.* The objectives of its graduate program must be defined by each institution for itself, in clear recognition of its resources and its other commitments. The definition of purposes needs to express two decisions: the subject matter or professional areas in which graduate work will be made available, and the changes the program seeks to induce in the minds of the students who embark upon it.

2. *The separate identity of the program.* A good graduate program is a recognizable entity. Its faculty has a sense of permanence and identity, under the leadership of a dean or director of its own who knows graduate work and has time to help build a consistent long range program. Its students benefit by the stimulation of a community of inquiring minds with common interests but diverse backgrounds; this is the point at which a very small graduate program is apt to lack vitality, and is also a justification for requiring a substantial period of full time resident work for an advanced degree.

3. *Faculty qualifications and interests.* Instructors who are responsible for graduate teaching should normally hold the highest terminal degrees or clear equivalents in their fields, plus whatever academic, professional, or practical experience the nature of their teaching requires. But their scholarship must not be static. They should be so interested in the frontiers of knowledge that they enjoy research and creativity for their own sake and constantly pursue them. They should be encouraged by teaching schedules favorable to research, by all the facilities and aids the institution can provide, and by salary and promotion plans which emphasize scholarly and creative productivity.

4. *Teaching assignments.* While the graduate faculty should be an identifiable entity, its members need not be restricted to advanced instruction. Their competence and influence is often valuable in the undergraduate courses also. By distributing the teaching assignments an institution provides a richer sequence of advanced courses than it could if it limited its offerings to the areas in which it could maintain full time graduate specialists. The instructors benefit by wider professional contacts, and both graduate and undergraduate students gain the advantage of a greater variety of points of view. But graduate instruction requires so much time for preparation, for guidance and research counseling, and for the instructor's own creative work that each course and student he directs has to be counted as more than a numerically equivalent undergraduate load. Graduate teaching can be part of a normal schedule which includes undergraduate teaching, but it can not be added to a full program of undergraduate work without vitiating both. Extra compensation is no solution. The instructor's time is the limiting factor. In the long run the stimulating quality of the teaching and research guidance are the elements which more than any others determine the worth of a graduate program.

5. *Student selection.* The mastery of knowledge which a good graduate program requires is possible only for a student of ability, perseverance, and scholarly interest who can build his advanced studies upon good preparation. Graduate admission should therefore require substantial evidence of both aptitude and academic achievement. Possession of a baccalaureate degree is not enough.

Since graduate students do not work in a vacuum but are stimulated or depressed by the level of activity of their fellows, selective admission should apply to graduate courses as well as to degree candidacy. It is poor practice to mix casual or unproved students in classes with serious candidates, for they inevitably affect the pace and intensity of the work. This is particularly a danger in late afternoon, evening, and extension courses.

6. *The nature of graduate courses.* On the other hand the distinction between advanced undergraduate and initial graduate courses need not be so sharp that it prohibits admitting an occasional undergraduate to a graduate course for which he is really qualified. The underlying principle ought to be that all graduate courses are designed for graduate students. If some others can take advantage of them to their own profit and without hindering the graduate group, they should be encouraged to do so.

Since graduate study at the master's level should give the student an awareness of the ramifications of his subject in related fields, it will be desirable in some cases to introduce him to ancillary disciplines in which he has not had previous training. It is possible, with care, to construct special introductory courses for this purpose and to present them in a manner which warrants graduate credit. The instructor must assume in graduate students an intellectual maturity, habits of scholarship, intensity of effort and general background greater than those commonly shown by undergraduates. It is proper and often desirable to admit advanced undergraduates who have such qualities to these courses also, thereby meeting similar needs on their part and providing a large enough group to support the course. It is poor practice to give graduate credit for undergraduate courses augmented by special assignments.

7. *The unity of a student's program.* A graduate degree program needs comprehensiveness and unity. It must also fit the particular background of the indi-

vidual and help him achieve his own aims. The resultant combination of discipline and flexibility implies firm curriculum principles, great adaptability in their application, consistent and informed guidance; it also implies a means whereby all the facets of the student's work may at the end be brought to a focus and the extent to which he has achieved his objectives assessed. A well designed comprehensive examination can do this in a master's program. It should be broader than the courses the student has taken and may well extend beyond them, for its purpose is to clarify and appraise his orientation in the field as a whole. Such an examination should be prepared and the results read by several instructors who together represent the general field. Parts of it could be alike for all the candidates at a given time in a particular subject area.

8. *Research.* Doctoral work invariably requires original research or experimentation, the results of which are set forth in writing and defended orally. The expectation at the master's level is not as uniform, because master's programs may differ considerably in kind, but in every type substantial experience in the scholar's approach to the acquisition, preparation, and analysis of information is indispensable.

A thesis is the device normally used when the master's course is designed to be an introduction to or preparation for research. Creative work or distinguished performance involving intellectual as well as technical mastery may appropriately be substituted in the arts, music, and literature. In such applied areas as teaching and engineering a sequence of investigations of the professional literature and practice or a solution of a complex problem is sometimes used to good effect.

The essential element is independent work in depth, whatever its form. Whether it is carried out in connection with courses or not is immaterial if the project forces the student to work on his own and to learn how to find and treat his materials in a scholarly manner.

9. *The library.* Graduate study in any field, even more than undergraduate, is dependent upon the library. It requires resources out of proportion to the additional number of courses and students concerned. Not only must the advanced courses be supported with a greater number and more specialized kinds of books, monographs, source materials, periodicals, and reference works in the field of instruction and related areas, but the background material for many special investigations will be demanded too. Lack of superior library resources or failure to use them well condemns the program to mediocrity at the start.

OFF-CAMPUS GRADUATE COURSES

Off-campus graduate work presents formidable difficulties, for the instruction and resources offered graduate students, indeed any students, in extension courses should be educationally equal in every respect to those enjoyed by resident students. If graduate courses are given in extension they should be of such unquestionable quality that there need be no restriction on applying their credits toward degrees, although a substantial period of study in an established, permanently staffed center should be required of degree candidates to give them the advantage of association with other advanced students.

One safeguard for the quality of off-campus courses is to have them set up, controlled, and supervised through the same departmental, faculty, and administrative channels as other courses and taught by full time members of the faculty as part of their normal loads.

It takes a mature, skilled instructor to make advanced study exciting and rewarding for men and women who have just finished a day's work. He can not use a prefabricated course: he must sense at his first session what will fit the needs of his diversified and critical group and select and adapt his material on the spot. The use of casual instructors and the assigning of graduate extension courses to regular faculty members as an additional responsibility for extra pay is indefensible in any but emergency or other exceptional circumstances.

Extension graduate courses should require as much and as high a level of preparation and outside reading as campus courses do. If late afternoon, evening, and weekend courses are to do so, employed students who take them must limit their registrations accordingly, in proportion to the other demands upon their time and strength. Furthermore, superior library resources must be available for extension students at times and in places which favor their use. It is not sufficient to bring a few books from the campus collection, to depend on local public libraries, or to expect extension students to travel to the campus library when it is necessary to bring the course itself to them. The institution will have to purchase duplicates of many volumes in the central library for the extension center.

Sometimes several institutions pooling their resources can provide a better cooperative extension program than any of them could singly.

THE COST OF GRADUATE WORK

It need hardly be added that graduate work is expensive. An institution should not deceive itself by thinking it can have a high caliber graduate program on a self-supporting basis. The additional students it attracts will not absorb its cost. Graduate instructors teach fewer classes; fewer students are enrolled in them; much individual counseling is necessary; and additional facilities and frequently expensive equipment are required. An institution with a graduate program needs a larger staff than it would have without it, for a satisfactory graduate program can not be developed by adding responsibilities to persons who already have a full schedule of undergraduate teaching. Its library budget is markedly increased.

Before an institution begins offering graduate courses it should assess carefully and realistically the effects the move will have on its undergraduate program, and know where the necessary additional resources are to come from.

North Central Association of Colleges and Secondary Schools

"Policy on the Accreditation of Doctoral Programs"

. . . In the paragraphs which follow the Commission on Colleges and Universities of the North Central Association has outlined a procedure for the accreditation of doctoral programs which it feels will halt any erosion of quality at the level of the doctorate.

1. To begin with, we feel that more time, energy, and considered judgment must be utilized in conducting an examination of doctoral work. . . . More details regarding faculty training, faculty publications, faculty research, and faculty experience in the direction of advanced work should be called for and studied meticulously before an accreditation visit is begun. A full examination of library and laboratory resources is essential. . . .

5. The examiners should of course take into account not only major fields which are proposed for the doctoral program but also supporting fields. Practically no curricular area is self-sufficient. A staff which is not sustained by colleagues in related areas cannot be expected to carry on the training of advanced students.

6. Particular attention should be devoted to the qualifications of the faculty. The visiting team should take into account (a) the doctoral training of each staff member who is to participate in the program; (b) the scholarly activities in which he has previously engaged; (c) the list of his publications during the past ten years and where and in what form these appeared; (d) the scholarly projects or plans which he is at present pursuing; and, in general (e) his scholarly stature insofar as this can be determined. It is our considered opinion that no departmental Ph.D. program can be justified unless the group conducting it includes at least three members who are actively engaged in research and publication.

7. A detailed examination of the library holdings in the areas under consideration should be made . . . and the laboratory equipment and other physical facilities should likewise be considered in detail, as should the space available for graduate students and for those who are to direct them. . . .

9. The examiners should consider the proposed pattern of graduate enrollment, to learn particularly the extent to which graduate students will or will not be mixed with undergraduates, the kind of work designed especially for doctoral students, the number of seminars to be made available and whether these are true seminars, most of all the opportunities which each student will have to receive individual faculty attention. The examiners should also ascertain whether the requirements for admission to candidacy are sufficiently high and whether the student is held to the acquisition of certain skills such as a knowledge of statistics or of foreign languages or bibliographic techniques.

Northwest Association of Secondary and Higher Schools

"Guide for Self-Evaluation and Accreditation of Higher Schools"

SELF EVALUATION REPORT III

. . . Naturally the facilities available in a small institution giving a few master's degrees each year will not match those in a larger institution offering the doctoral degree in several areas. Nevertheless the institution, regardless of the size of its program, should be able to show that its graduate program is distinct from its undergraduate program in respect to admission policies, scholastic requirements, course offerings, etc. The institution should be able to show that its graduate program represents a separate and distinct activity.

A. *Objectives*
Report:

1. The particular objectives of the graduate program of the institution over and above those described in SELF-EVALUATION REPORT I and II.
(A mere accretion of courses beyond the baccalaureate degree does not constitute a graduate program.)

2. Studies made recently, looking to a review of these objectives.

3. The extent to which these objectives can be carried out by the institution with its present programs, organization, and resources.

4. Any other activities of the institution, such as museums, observatories, research institutes, etc., and their relation to the educational objectives of this program.

B. *Evidence of Stability*
Report:

1. The history of the growth and development of the graduate program.

2. Names of administrative directors of the graduate program during the last ten years, with period of service of each.

3. Yearly enrollments in the graduate programs in tabular form for the last ten years, with summer session and extension courses listed separately.

C. *Finance*
Report:

Special funds allocated to the development and support of the graduate program. . . .

D. *Plant*

Physical plant facilities . . . should be presented here if not adequately covered elsewhere.

E. *Materials and Equipment*
Report:

1. A tabulation of total value of equipment and the value of acquisitions during the past three years, if not already adequately covered in SELF-EVALUATION REPORT I and II.

F. *Library*

The information requested in REPORT I (pp. 9-10) is not adequate for the evaluation of library facilities for graduate work. In addition to the data there requested:

Report over-all institutional library facilities not reported in REPORT I. . . .

1. The holdings of multivolume *encyclopedic compilations* (e.g., Inter-

162

national Critical Tables, Beilstein, Encyclopedia of Social Sciences, Cambridge History of English Literature, Dictionary of American Biography, etc.)

2. The holdings of abstract journals (e.g., Chemical Abstracts . . .)

3. The holdings of other specialized research periodicals (e.g., American Journal of Physiology, vv. 10-99 (1901-1947), American Political Science Review, Publications of the Modern Language Association of America)

4. The holdings of general or non-specialized research journals (e.g., Hand. d. Koninklijke Akademia van Wetenschappen, 26-91) (1892-1938)

5. Any other significant library facilities, bearing directly upon graduate work in any of the fields concerned (e.g., collections of manuscript material, cuneiform tablets, Northwest history, etc.)

6. List special arrangements for intensive use of library facilities (e.g., stack carrels, hours of availability in general library and in divisional or departmental libraries. . . .)

G. *Records and Reports*
Report:

1. Records other than those centralized in the offices of the Registrar, Business Office, Alumni Office, Placement Office, Health Service, etc.

2. Whether copies of theses are kept in the library, and if so, whether they are available on interlibrary loan.

3. Whether the institution publishes periodically a volume of abstracts of theses, and if so, how frequently.

4. Whether a record is kept of the publications of these theses in national journals, and if so, about what per cent is published in each graduate field.

H. *The Curriculum*
Report:

1. For each department, indicate the major fields of specialization for both the master's degree and the doctorate.

2. Courses used for graduate credit by submitting a college catalog in which each of these courses has been checked.

3. For each graduate degree (M.A., M.S., M.Ed., Ph.D., Ed.D., etc.) the credit requirements in major field and minor field(s), experience, academic standing and residence requirements, maximum credits that may be carried at one time, what if any off-campus extension credits may be applied towards a master's degree. What limit is set upon the use of short-time or working credits toward an advanced degree. Tabulate wherever possible, and where variation occurs between departments for the same degree, explain in footnotes.

4. Professional degrees (M.E., E.E., etc.) awarded on the basis of experience, with or without a "thesis," should be reported.

5. How additional graduate offerings or graduate degrees are authorized or existing programs discontinued.

I. The Instructional Staff

Report:

1. Personnel

   a. For each department offering major graduate work, list members of the faculty authorized to direct theses of major students and how they are selected.

2. Organization

   a. If the institution has a graduate faculty, what is its authority, functions and responsibilities.

3. Teaching load

   Report:

   What recognition in terms of teaching load is given by the several departments for the direction of student research and the preparation of graduate theses.

J. Instruction. . . .

1. List additional features characteristic of or peculiar to the graduate program. In particular what special facilities are available for the improvement of instruction and for professional development (graduate seminars, interdepartmental seminars, graduate honor societies, travel funds for staff attending professional meetings, etc.).

2. Student Achievement

   Report:

   a. Percentage of students dropped from graduate program for poor scholarship during their first academic year.

   b. Percentage not dropped but otherwise disciplined for poor scholarship during their first academic year. What disciplinary measures were employed?

3. What per cent of a student's program is devoted to the thesis.

4. Under what conditions is a thesis not required.

5. What per cent of a student's program must be "residence" work. (Give residence requirements and definition of residence in institution concerned.)

6. Time limit for completion of the work required for an advanced degree.

K. Administration

The following information is requested with reference to the administration of the graduate program.

Report:

1. Who canvasses the field for candidates, who makes recommendations, who is consulted, and who is the final appointing authority when a new dean or executive officer is selected for the graduate program, division, or school.

2. By name, the personnel of the "graduate council" or other administrative group responsible for graduate work, showing the field, school, or department each represents. How each is selected, and for what length of time.

3. The frequency of meetings of this group.

4. The authority exercised by this group.

5. Number and function of any other committees operating in connection with the graduate program.

6. Procedure for approving a staff member to offer major graduate work.

L. *The Students*

. . . The following data should be supplied for graduate students.

Report:

1. Baccalaureate origins of graduate students registered during current academic year.

2. The qualifications for admission as graduate students.

3. What officer or committee passes on such admissions.

4. When, how and by whom a student once admitted to the program is "advanced to candidacy."

5. How course schedules of students with baccalaureate degrees who are not presently following an advanced degree program are approved.

6. By what arrangement and with whose approval a student is assigned to a professor to direct his thesis.

7. In tabular form for each department offering graduate degrees: the number of major graduate students registered during the academic year reported including the preceding summer session. The number of master's and doctor's degrees conferred, and in which departmental specialty. (This report should cover each of the last five years.)

8. What limitation is put upon awarding degrees to staff members.

9. What limitation is put upon students securing all of their degrees from the institution.

10. For each department, the number of teaching assistantships, fellowships, etc., available on departmental funds, the number of similar positions available from other funds, and also the number of research assistantships and fellowships available from institutional and non-institutional funds.

11. The annual stipend (9 or 12 months) paid for each of the above classifications, the percentage of full-time position that each represents, also the fraction of full-time study that the holder of each appointment may carry.

12. How many postdoctoral fellows each department has had during the past five years.

Southern Association of Colleges and Schools

"Manual for the Institutional Self-Study and Periodic Visitation Program"

. . . Do the charter and stated purpose of the institution include provision for graduate degrees? Are the resources of the institution sufficient to meet the additional demands required for graduate study? Do these resources include a library and laboratories designed for graduate study with special facilities for individual research?

Describe the administration of the graduate school or any graduate program. Show the relationship of the administrative head to other administrative officers, to the other divisions of the institution, to the Graduate Council, and to the faculty members of departments involved.

Indicate the scope of the graduate offerings. Is a special curriculum designed in various departments for the graduate students? What percentage of the curriculum may consist of undergraduate courses? Are departmental faculties sufficiently large to create the atmosphere and intellectual stimulation which is an essential part of a graduate program? List by departments all faculty teaching graduate courses, showing highest earned degree and significant research and publications.

Indicate by chart the number in the past five years who have taken graduate degrees in each discipline or combination.

What is the faculty or Graduate Council's evaluation of library holdings for graduate purposes? Describe any areas that need improvement. Show what steps should be taken to correct these deficiencies. Is the special training, research, or experience of the graduate faculty or the faculty members engaged in graduate teaching sufficient to justify a program of graduate study?

Describe the program of graduate assistantships, fellowships, and the use of graduate students as instructors in the institution.

Is there a real need for the graduate program? Has the graduate program strengthened or weakened the undergraduate program? What are the strengths and weaknesses of the graduate program?

Is the curriculum for the master's degree a fifth-year program or is it a collection of courses without depth in one area? Are courses in minors or supporting departments of graduate level?

What is the general opinion of the total faculty as to the quality of and need for graduate study? Does any department or school offer a graduate program which is not part of the Graduate School? What is the faculty evaluation of this procedure?

Western College Association

"Graduate Programs"

. . . The following questions are designed to bring out information, not elsewhere presented, which will give the visiting committee adequate information regarding the general fitness of the institution to give work leading to graduate degrees . . .

I. GENERAL INFORMATION

1. Give name and title of the person principally responsible for this report.
2. This is a report on the program for what degrees?
3. In what departments or fields of study may a student major for this degree?
4. Describe briefly the administrative set-up for graduate work, giving the lines of authority and supervision.

II. PROGRAM

Unless the program is described adequately in the catalog or elsewhere (give complete reference), give the following information:

1. Describe the objectives of each program leading to a graduate degree.
2. The total number of units required for this degree.
3. The total number of units required as a full-time resident student.
4. The total number of transfer units that may be accepted.
5. The total number of units required in courses restricted to graduate students.
6. The total number of units permitted in off-campus or extension courses. May these be graduate courses, or are they limited to upper-division undergraduate courses?
7. What requirements do you place on students for some creative expression of their scholarship, such as a research thesis, the solution of some complex problem or design, the critical analysis of a problem or of the work of others, the production of some original artistic work, etc.? State the number of units allowed for this.

III. FACULTY

Describe the special competence of the faculty to direct and offer graduate programs in terms of such factors as the following: . . .

IV. STUDENTS

1. What are the admission qualifications for the program? Explain how they are administered.
2. What standards of scholarship and what examination procedures are required of students in order to stay in the program?
3. How do you evaluate progress and achievement?

V. INSTITUTIONAL RESOURCES

If you offer degrees beyond the Master's describe any special resources available for students pursuing these degrees, such as library facilities, laboratory or research facilities, endowments, grants, subsidized programs, fellowships, etc.

VI. SUMMARY

In summary, state what you consider the main strengths and limitations of your program, and what steps are being taken to correct the latter.

1. Training and experience.
2. Load (instructional and advisory).
3. Competence to direct research.

The University of the State of New York

The University of the State of New York (the state department of education), while obviously not a regional association, is nevertheless one of the most comprehensive "accrediting" agencies in the world. In order to evaluate the effectiveness of graduate education, the Commissioner is currently studying a regulatory code which, when finally approved, will be employed in the State's evaluative procedures. The following tentative draft is reproduced here with approval from the Commissioner's office (Draft Number 2: January 2, 1962).

1. The following regulations governing the approval of graduate work shall apply to all courses of study in colleges and universities except those that lead to examination or certification for professional practice.

2. *Purpose.*

   a. The offering of graduate work shall be consonant with the announced and chartered purposes of the institution.

   b. Evidence shall be available concerning the broad objectives and the underlying conception of the graduate offerings.

3. *Resources.* General resources must be adequate to conduct a graduate program without diminution of the quality of any undergraduate curriculum offered.

4. *Administration.*

   a. The graduate program normally shall have administrative identity as an educational unit, and be headed by a dean or director. Small colleges without such a unit and head may apply for the registration of programs in individual disciplines leading to the master's degree.

   b. The administrative duties of a dean or director shall be devoted to the development and operation of the graduate school. He shall have had experience suited to the conduct of a graduate program and to the development of the appropriate courses of study.

   c. The development of educational policy shall be the responsibility of faculty members teaching on the graduate level acting under the leadership of the unit head.

   d. Evidence shall be available concerning the leadership and process for the development and screening of new programs and for the modification of those in existence.

5. *Faculty.*

   a. Staff members who teach at the graduate level normally shall hold the highest earned degree, or its equivalent, in their fields of instruction.

   b. A suitable number of full-time faculty members shall be maintained for effective presentation of the fields of specialization. A satisfactory faculty-student ratio shall be maintained in all classes and for the supervision of student programs at all degree levels.

   c. A majority of the faculty having full charge of graduate classes shall hold the rank of associate professor or above.

   d. A climate favorable to scholarly productivity shall be established. Arrangement of teaching commitments to provide time for study and research and establishment of a sabbatical leave policy are means to that end.

6. *Library.* An institution shall maintain a professionally administered library, in which there is a core of works, including books, periodicals, and primary sources, essential for adequate research and original investigation at the level of the degree and in the fields offered for instruction. Annual financial provision for the improvement of these resources is essential.

7. *Laboratory Facilities.* A graduate program shall have adequate laboratory and other special facilities necessary for the courses offered and research undertaken.

8. *Admission.* A graduate program shall require for admission a baccalaureate degree, or the equivalent. The applicant shall give evidence of capacity to pursue advanced studies successfully in the subject selected.

9. *Courses of Study.*

   a. Enrollment in individual courses offered for graduate credit shall be restricted primarily to graduate students.

   b. Programs shall be so designed as to give evidence of providing a level of mastery of the field appropriate to the degree and so as to constitute a carefully considered plan showing unity, depth, and cohesiveness. The design should be such that at appropriate times the various facets of a student's work may be brought together and the extent to which he has achieved his purposes may be assessed.

   c. The doctoral program shall require the student to do a creditable piece of scholarly research or to make an independent investigation of a topic of significance to the field of study.

   d. Candidates for the Ph.D. degree shall demonstrate capacity to use at least one foreign language as an instrument of research.

10. *Full-time graduate student.*

    a. A full-time graduate student is defined as one who is registered for twelve semester hours credit or its equivalent in the discretion of the Commissioner of Education. "Equivalent" as defined here shall normally mean independent study or research, supervised and approved by the graduate school in fulfillment of the requirements toward a graduate degree.

b. Institutions shall define and publish policies governing the employment of graduate students as assistants in instruction and/or research.

11. *Advising.*

a. Faculty members holding full-time teaching appointments shall normally be designated to carry out the advising of students with regard to programs.

b. Student programs of study shall be approved on a basis consonant with the published requirements of the institution.

c. The steps in progress toward the degree and requirements to be met by the students shall be clearly defined and published. Adequate provision should be made to record student progress toward achievement of the degree requirements.

12. *Outcomes.* Records shall normally be available to indicate the degree of acceptance of the graduates of the program by scholarly, research, educational, business, and governmental agencies.

APPENDIX V

Selected Bibliography

Abernathy, R., "National Conference on Graduate Study in Health Education, Physical Education, and Recreation." *Journal of Health–Physical Education–Recreation.* 20:645+, Dec., 1949.

Ackerlund, G. C., "Graduate Education Program: A Point of View." *Pennsylvania School Journal.* 106:129, Dec., 1957. Also, Dwyer, J. A., "Graduate Education Program: Another Point of View." *Ibid.,* 106:333, April, 1958.

American Psychological Association. *Graduate education in psychology. Report of the conference.* Washington, The Association, 1959. 97p.

Anderson, W. W. and Richardson, O. T., "Bases for Evaluating the Master's Program." *Journal of Higher Education.* 24:376-81, Oct., 1953.

"Are Graduate Schools Slighting a Major Function?" *Carnegie Corporation Quarterly.* 8, No. 1:1-3, Jan., 1960.

Armentrout, W. D., "First Year of the Advanced Professional Program for Teachers." *Peabody Journal of Education.* 29:130-35, Nov., 1951.

Ashida, M. E. and Bernd, D. W., "Whence the New Professors? Reply to R. E. Knoll." *College English.* 21:49, Oct., 1959.

Association of American Universities. Committee on Graduate Work. "The Master's Degrees." In: *Journal of Proceedings and Addresses.* 1945. pp. 111-25.

Association of Graduate Schools. "Report of Committee on Policies in Graduate Education." In: *Journal of Proceedings and Addresses.* Eleventh Annual Conference, 1959. pp. 36-43.

Axelrod, Joseph, ed., *Graduate study for future college teachers.* Washington, American Council on Education, 1959. 111p.

Axinn, G. H., "Rigor in Cooperative Extension Graduate Research." *Adult Education.* 10, No. 4:234-37, Summer, 1960.

Axt, Richard G., *Research on graduate education: Report of a conference.* Washington, Brookings Institution, 1959. 108p.

Baker, C., "Needs in the Graduate School." *College English.* 11:339-44, March, 1950.

Barr, A. S., "State-wide Co-operation in Teacher Education." *Journal of Teacher Education.* 11:447-48, Sept., 1960.

Barzun, Jacques, "The Degrees, the Pace, the Product." In: *The Carnegie conference on higher education: Addresses and discussions,* 1957. New York, Carnegie Corporation, 1958. pp. 130-40.

Beach, L. B., "Freedom and Discipline in Graduate Programs." *Journal of Higher Education.* 30:120-23, March, 1959.

———, "What Should Be the Role of the Master's Degree in the Preparation of College Teachers?" In: Association for Higher Education. *Current issues in higher education,* 1960. (Edited by G. Kerry Smith.) Washington, National Education Association, 1960. pp. 187-89.

Beck, H. P., *Men who control our universities.* New York, King's Crown Press, 1947. viii, 229p.

Bent, H. E., "Administration of Graduate Schools." *Higher Education.* 8:17-18, Sept. 15, 1951.

Bentley, G. B., "Graduate School as a Preparation for Teachers." *College English.* 12:330-35, March, 1951.

Berelson, Bernard, *Graduate education in the United States.* New York, McGraw-Hill, 1960. vi, 346p.

———, "Perspective on Graduate Education." *School and Society.* 89:139-41, March 25, 1961.

Blegen, Theodore C., "Ferment in Graduate Education." In: Department of Higher Education. *Analysts' addresses. Companion volume to current issues in higher education,* 1950. Washington, National Education Association, 1950. pp. 44-50.

———, "Graduate Schools and the Education of College Teachers." *Educational Record.* 29:12-25, Jan., 1948. Bibliography.

Blegen, Theodore C. and Cooper, Russell M., eds., *The preparation of college teachers.* Washington, American Council on Education, 1950. 186p.

Blessing, James H., *Graduate education: An annotated bibliography.* (U. S. Office of Education. Bulletin 1961, No. 26.) Washington, U. S. Government Printing Office, 1961. vi, 151p.

Board of Control for Southern Regional Education, *Improving graduate education: A guide to institutional self-evaluation.* Atlanta, Ga., The Board, 1951. 117p.

Boewe, Charles E. and Nichols, Ray F., eds., *Both human and humane: The humanities and social sciences in graduate education.* Philadelphia, University of Pennsylvania Press, 1960. 224p.

Bond, J. M., "Some Aspects of Graduate and Professional Education for Negroes." *Phylon.* 10, No. 4:392-96, 1949.

Bowers, D. F. and Greene, T. M., "Graduate Work in Philosophy." *Journal of Higher Education.* 16:178-88, April, 1945.

Boyd, G. H., "Accreditation Program and Its Significance to the Graduate School." *Southern Association Quarterly.* 12:104-7, Feb., 1948.

Bretsch, H. S. and Stowe, A. R. M., "Theses, Not Thesis." *Educational Research Bulletin.* 29:126-32, May, 1950.

Brickman, William W., "M. A. and the Ph.D." *School and Society.* 66:169-74, Aug. 30, 1947. Bibliography.

Brigham, R. J., "Provisions for Graduate Work for Negroes in Missouri." *Journal of Negro Education.* 16:242-46, April, 1947.

Brogan, Albert P., "Restoring the Master's Degree." *Graduate Journal.* 1:34-40, Spring, 1958.

Brown, A., "Graduate and Professional Education in Negro Institutions." *Journal of Negro Education.* 27, No. 3:233-42, Summer, 1958. Bibliography.

Brubacher, John S. and Rudy, Willis, *Higher education in transition: An American history: 1636-1956.* New York, Harper, 1958. 494p.

Brumbaugh, Aaron J. and Blee, Myron R., *Higher education and Florida's future.* Prepared for the Council for the Study of Higher Education in Florida. (Volume 5 deals with graduate education in the arts and sciences.) Gainesville, University of Florida Press, 1956. 5v.

Bryant, L. C., "Graduate Training in Negro Colleges." *Journal of Negro Education.* 30, No. 1:69-71, Winter, 1961.

Buell, I. A., "Master's Degree." *American Association of University Professors Bulletin.* 30:400-405, Sept., 1944.

——, "Small College and the Master's Degree." *Journal of Higher Education.* 15:413-20, Nov., 1944.

Bunting, J. W., "Industry and the Graduate School." *Educational Record.* 40:301-11, Oct., 1959.

Butler, Raymond S., "Interinstitutional Cooperation in Higher Education." *School and Society.* 87:44-47, Jan. 31, 1959.

Butterweck, Joseph S., "Master's Degree for Teachers." *Peabody Journal of Education.* 38:292-302, March, 1961.

——, "A Post-Baccalaureate Program in General Education." *Liberal Education.* 47:483-91, Dec., 1961.

Calkins, R. D., "Professional and Graduate Education and the Liberal Arts." In: Conference on Liberal Arts. *Proceedings,* 1952. pp. 48-64. Bibliography.

Campbell, George W., "University Extension Centers in Higher Education." *Teachers College Record.* 59:156-62, Dec., 1957.

Carmichael, Oliver C., *Graduate education: A critique and a program.* New York, Harper, 1961.

Cartwright, W. H., "Graduate Education of Teachers; Proposals for the Future." *Educational Record.* 40:148-54, April, 1959.

Chambers, M. M., "Ideas Versus Organization: Practical Matters." *Graduate Journal.* 3:130-38, Spring, 1960.

Cohen, N. E., "Future of Graduate Training for Social Work." *Educational Record.* 32:142-51, April, 1951. Bibliography.

Commission on Human Resources and Advanced Training. *America's resources of specialized talent: A current appraisal and a look ahead.* Report prepared by Dael Wolfle, director. New York, Harper, 1954. xviii, 332p.

Committee on Subdoctoral Education of the Education and Training Board. "The Training of Technical Workers in Psychology at the Subdoctoral Level." *American Psychologist.* 10:541-45, 1955.

Conference of University Administrators on General and Liberal Education. *Report of proceedings,* 1944. Washington, J. P. Blickensderfer, 1944. 200p.

Cooper, R. M. and others, "Educational Program: Purposes and Programs." *Review of Educational Research.* 30:339-41, Oct., 1960. Bibliography.

Cowley, W. H., "Three Curricular Conflicts." *Liberal Education.* 46:467-83, Dec., 1960.

Crall, H. W. and Myers, R. M., "Recommendation for Master's Degree Preparation for Teachers of Biological Sciences." *Journal of Teacher Education.* 11:506-11, Dec., 1960. Bibliography.

Curtin, W. R., "Requirements for the Master's Degree with a Major in Education." *Catholic Educational Review.* 57:73-96, 145-61, Feb.-March, 1959. Bibliography.

Cutts, Norma E., ed., *School psychologists at mid-century.* (The Thayer Conference Report.) Washington, American Psychological Association, 1955. ix, 230p.

De Loach, W. S., "Master's Degree Programs of a Group of High School Chemistry Teachers." *Journal of Educational Research.* 46:71-73, Sept., 1952.

Dougherty, C. T., "Graduate Education and the Preparation of College Teachers." *National Catholic Educational Association Bulletin.* 58:153-57, Aug., 1961.

Ducasse, C. J., "Graduate Preparation for Teaching." *Journal of Higher Education.* 19:443-47+, Dec., 1948.

Eckelberry, R. H., "Graduate Degrees as Professional Degrees." *Journal of Higher Education.* 30:172-73, March, 1959.

Edwards, Marcia, *Studies in American graduate education.* New York, Carnegie Foundation for the Advancement of Teaching, 1944. 71p.

Eells, Walter Crosby, *College teachers and college teaching: An annotated bibliography.* Atlanta, Ga., Southern Regional Conference Board, 1957. 282p. *Supplement,* 1959. 134p.

————, "Leading American Graduate Schools." *Association of American Colleges Bulletin.* 43:563-76, Dec., 1957.

Elder, J. P., *A criticism of the Graduate School of Arts and Sciences in Harvard University and Radcliffe College.* Cambridge, Mass., Harvard University Graduate School, 1958. 48p.

————, "Reviving the Master's Degree for the Prospective College Teacher." *Journal of Higher Education.* 30:133-36, March, 1959.

Elkus, A. I., "Place of Applied Music in Graduate Study." *Music Educators Journal.* 32:30+, Jan., 1946.

Elvehjem, Conrad A., "Graduate Work—A Thirty-Five Year Experience." In: *Proceedings of the Midwest Conference on Graduate Study and Research.* 15th Annual Meeting, 1959. pp. 49-52.

Ertell, Merton W., *Interinstitutional cooperation in higher education: A study of experiences with reference to New York State.* Albany, University of the State of New York, 1957. 118p.

Fairman, C., "Experiment in Graduate Instruction." *American Association of University Professors Bulletin.* 33:640-47, Dec., 1947.

Fisher, J. J., "Experiment in Graduate Education." *Association of American Colleges Bulletin.* 43:286-89, May, 1957.

Fitzroy, Herbert W. K., "How and To What Extent Can Higher Institutions within the Same Community Coordinate Their Efforts in the Interests of Efficiency and Economy?" In: Association for Higher Education. *Current issues in higher education,* 1958. (Edited by G. Kerry Smith.) Washington, National Education Association, 1958. pp. 152-63.

————, "The Richmond Area University Center: An Experiment in Cooperation." *Educational Record.* 38:241-49, July, 1957.

Fleege, U. H., "Program of General Education and the Graduate School." *Journal of General Education.* 3:26-33, Oct., 1948.

Fleming, W., "Wanted: New Program for the Preparation of College Teachers in Art and Music." *Journal of General Education.* 3:107-12, Jan., 1949.

Forbes, J. D., "Note on the Master of Arts Degree." *Journal of Higher Education.* 18:432-34, Nov., 1947.

Friedenberg, E. Z. and Roth, J. A., *Self-perception in the university*. Chicago, University of Chicago Press, 1954. vii, 102p.

Funkhouser, W. D., "Conference on Graduate Work in Negro Institutions in the South." *Journal of Negro Education*. 15:122-27, Jan., 1946.

Galfo, A. J., "M.Ed. Degree: What Kind of Graduate Study Should It Encompass?" *Virginia Journal of Education*. 54:19+, March, 1961.

Gardner, E. F., *Tomorrow's graduate school of education*. Syracuse, N. Y., Syracuse University Press, 1958. 60p.

Gaskill, A. R., "We Now Offer the Master's Degree." *Teachers College Journal*. 28:6-8, Oct., 1956.

Gibbs, W. T., "Problems in Negro Graduate Schools." *Quarterly Review of Higher Education Among Negroes*. 13:371-76, Oct., 1945.

"Graduate Education in the United States." *Education Digest*. 26:42-44, Jan., 1961.

"Graduate Study for Faculty Members." *Higher Education*. 13:28, Oct., 1956.

"Graduate Training for College Teaching: A Panel Discussion." *AAUP Bulletin*. 46:294-99, Sept., 1960.

Graduate training in economics. A report on panel discussions at Yale. New Haven, Conn., Yale University Press, 1956.

"Graduate Work in Negro Institutions." *Higher Education*. 2:8-9, Jan. 1, 1946.

"Graduate Work in Summer Session." In: *Proceedings of the Midwest Conference on Graduate Study and Research*. 13th Annual Meeting, 1957. pp. 30-34.

Grigg, Charles M., *Who wants to go to graduate school, and why? Research reports in social science*, V. 2, No. 1. Tallahassee, Fla., Center for Social Research, Florida State University, 1959. 27p.

Grinnell, J. E., "Problem of the Mediocre Graduate Student." *Peabody Journal of Education*. 35:131-36, Nov., 1957.

Gropper, George L. and Fitzpatrick, Robert, *Who goes to graduate school?* Pittsburgh, Pa., American Institute for Research, 1959. 66p.

Guerry, A., "Accreditation of Graduate Instruction in the South, the Liberal Arts College, and College Teaching." *Southern Association Quarterly*. 12:107-9, Feb., 1948.

Gustavson, R. G., "Graduate Education for Research." Association of Graduate Schools. *Journal of Proceedings*. 1949:41-52.

Hamilton, H. A., "Present Status of Higher Education for Business." *American Business Education Yearbook*. 1957:30-46. Bibliography.

Hammond, L. M., "Master's Degree Program." *Association of American Colleges Bulletin*. 44:65-70, March, 1958.

Hanson, Henry P., *Self-evaluation reports III: Graduate school*. Corvallis, Ore., Oregon State College, 1960.

Hedrick, J. A. and William, C. S., "Negroes in Southern Graduate Education." *Phi Delta Kappan*. 36:102-104+, Nov., 1954.

Henry, David D., "Encouraging Research and Graduate Work." *School and Society*. 86:107, March 1, 1958.

Herskovits, M. J., "Some Problems of Graduate Training in Anthropology." *American Anthropologist*. 51:517-23, July, 1949.

Hewitt, J. E., "Requirements for the Master's Degree in Physical Education." *Journal of Health–Physical Education–Recreation*. 16:369-70+, Sept., 1945.

"Higher Education: The Graduate School." *Southern Association Quarterly.* 11:564-71, Aug., 1947.

Hilgard, E. R., "General Education at the Graduate Level." *Journal of Higher Education.* 26:294-97, June, 1955.

Hodenfield, G. K. and Stinnett, T. M., *The education of teachers: Conflict and consensus.* New York, Prentice-Hall, 1961. 177p.

Holden, W. P., Jr., "Master of Arts in Teaching at Yale, 1951-58." *Journal of Teacher Education.* 10:393-400, Dec., 1959.

Hollis, Ernest V., *Toward improving Ph.D. programs.* Washington, American Council on Education, 1945. xii, 204p.

Hoover, C. B., "Report of the Committee on Graduate Instruction." In: Southern University Conference. *Proceedings,* 1947. pp. 116-29.

Horner, J. E., "Dangerous Trends in Graduate Education." *Journal of Higher Education.* 30:167-68, March, 1959.

Hughes, R. M., *Manual for trustees of colleges and universities.* Ames, Iowa, Iowa State College Press, 1945. ix, 172p.

Hunter, J. M., "Evaluation of Graduate Work Offered by Negro Colleges." *Quarterly Review of Higher Education Among Negroes.* 15:338-47, Oct., 1947.

Institute for Administrative Officers of Higher Institutions. *Administration of higher institutions under changing conditions.* Chicago, University of Chicago Press, 1947.

———, *Problems of faculty personnel.* Chicago, University of Chicago Press, 1946.

Ivey, J. E., Jr., "Regional Graduate Education in the South." *Journal of Higher Education.* 22:97-98, Feb., 1951.

———, "Regional Plans Developed for Graduate Study and Research." *Nation's Schools.* 46:68, Nov., 1950.

Jaracz, W. A., "Trends in Graduate Education." *Higher Education.* 11:87-89, Feb., 1955.

Jenkins, L. W., "Master Teachers: Program of Graduate Study." *Clearing House.* 23:9-11, Sept., 1948.

Jones, Howard Mumford, *American humanism: Its meaning for world survival.* New York, Harper, 1957. 108p.

———, "Direction and Future Responsibility of Graduate Training." In: Southern University Conference. *Proceedings,* 1947. pp. 103-15.

———, *Education and world tragedy.* Cambridge, Mass., Harvard University Press, 1946. viii, 178p.

———, "Graduate School and the Problems of Training Teachers." Association of Graduate Schools. *Journal of Proceedings.* 1949:52-75.

———, *One great society: Humane learning in the United States.* New York, Harcourt, Brace, 1959. 241p.

Jones, L. M., "Graduate Minor in Physical Education." *Research Quarterly.* 19:18-21, March, 1948.

Jordan, J. C., "Problems Facing Graduate Education in the South." *Southern Association Quarterly.* 11:294-304, May, 1947.

Kandel, Isaac L., "Graduate Studies in Teaching and Research." *School and Society.* 69:53, Jan. 22, 1949.

Kazamias, A. M., "Education of Good Teachers and the Oberlin Master of Arts in Teaching Program." *Journal of Teacher Education.* 12:205-8, June, 1961.

Keezer, Dexter M., ed., *Financing higher education: 1960-1970.* New York, Mc-Graw-Hill, 1959. 304p.

Keniston, Hayward, *Graduate study and research in the arts and sciences at the University of Pennsylvania.* The educational survey of the University of Pennsylvania. Philadelphia, University of Pennsylvania Press, 1959. 150p.

Kirk, Grayson, "It Takes a Person Too Long To Get an Advanced Degree." *Nation's Schools.* 64:50, July, 1959.

Klapper, Paul, "Inflation in Educational Curricula." *School and Society.* 71:1-9, Jan. 7, 1950.

Knight, E. W. and Adams, A. B., eds., *Graduate school research and publications.* Chapel Hill, N. C., University of North Carolina Press, 1946.

Knowles, Asa S., "Emerging Features of Tomorrow's Higher Education." *Educational Record.* 38:329-39, Oct., 1957.

Koenker, Robert H., "Co-operative Graduate Programs." *Journal of Teacher Education.* 10, No. 4:507-12, Dec., 1959.

Korfmacher, W. C., "Graduate School: Last Citadel." *School and Society.* 77:257-59, April 25, 1953. Bibliography.

Kroepsch, Robert H., "Meeting New England's Higher Education Needs." *College and University.* 35:263-70, Spring, 1960.

Laframboise, M. A., "Master's Degree: Secondary or College Qualification?" *School Science and Mathematics.* 61:58-59, Jan., 1961.

Lessenger, W. E., "Patterns for Advanced Professional Work in Teacher Education." In: American Association of Colleges for Teacher Education. *Second yearbook,* 1949. pp. 60-64.

Lewis, H. F., "Liberal-Arts College in the Training of Scientists." *Journal of Higher Education.* 22:297-303+, June, 1951.

Leys, Wayne A. R., "Terminal Master's Degree." *Harvard Educational Review.* 26, No. 3:233-40, 1956. Bibliography.

Lindquist, Clarence B., ed., *Staffing the Nation's colleges and universities. Report of a conference, May 20 and 21, 1957.* Washington, U. S. Department of Health, Education, and Welfare, 1957. 59p.

Lindvall, Frederick C., "Post-graduate Engineering Education in Industry and the Community." *Journal of Engineering Education.* 48:701-7+, May, 1958.

Little, J. Kenneth, "Graduate Education." In: *Encyclopedia of educational research.* (Edited by Chester H. Harris for the American Educational Research Association.) New York, Macmillan, 1960. pp. 593-602.

Lloyd, R. G., "Some Problems of Graduate Schools Operated Primarily for Negroes." *Journal of Negro Education.* 25, No. 1:83-86, 1956.

Loehwing, Walter F., "A Graduate Dean Looks at the Summer Session." In: *Proceedings of the Midwest Conference on Graduate Study and Research.* 14th Annual Meeting, 1958. pp. 10-18.

Lomax, P. S., "Graduate Business Teacher Education." *National Business Education Quarterly.* 17:21-24, May, 1949.

Lowry, W. McNeill, "Institutional Cooperation in Higher Education." In: *Proceedings of the Midwest Conference on Graduate Study and Research.* 13th Annual Meeting, 1957. pp. 8-13.

Lumiansky, R. M., "Concerning Graduate Education for Teachers." *Educational Record.* 40:143-47, April, 1959.

Maaske, R. J., "Factors in a Desirable Master's Degree Program for Elementary School Teachers." *Educational Administration and Supervision.* 41:23-30, Jan., 1955.

McCloy, C. H., "A Letter to the Dean of the Graduate College." *Modern Language Journal.* 42:45-46, Jan., 1958.

McCoy, R. F., "Newer Developments in Master's Programs (Summary)." *National Catholic Educational Association Bulletin.* 56:183, Aug., 1959.

McCulloch, R. W., "Master's Degree." *School Review.* 64:55-56, Feb., 1956.

———, "Role of Graduate Schools in Teacher Education: A Study of Ten Graduate Programs." *North Central Association Quarterly.* 30:211-18, Oct., 1955.

McCutcheon, R. P., "Master's Degree and the Teacher Requirements." *School and Society.* 74:177-81, Sept. 22, 1951.

———, "Report of the Committee on Graduate Instruction." In: Southern University Conference. *Proceedings,* 1948. pp. 21-25.

McGill, E. C. and Winters, M., "Study of Thesis Requirements for the Master's Degree in Business Education." In: National Association of Business Teacher-Training Institutions. *Bulletin No. 48,* pp. 70-80.

McGlothlin, W. J., "Internships in Southern Graduate Programs." *Journal of Higher Education.* 20:83-87+, Feb., 1949.

McGrath, Earl J., *Graduate school and the decline of liberal education.* New York, Institute of Higher Education, Teachers College, Columbia University, 1959. 65p. Bibliography.

McGuire, M. R. P., "Recent Developments Regarding the Master's Degree." *National Catholic Educational Association Proceedings.* 1946:245-58.

Martin, T. B., "What Constitutes the Best Master's Degree Program?" *Business Education World.* 41:14-16, Dec., 1960.

Matthews, R. D., "Program of the Graduate Division." *Educational Outlook.* 24:200-205, May, 1950. Bibliography.

Matthewson, R. H., "Graduate Training for School Counselors." *Occupations.* 30:335-39, Feb., 1952. Bibliography.

Mays, A. B., "Problem of Graduate Study in Industrial Education." *Industrial Arts and Vocational Education.* 37:179-82, May, 1948.

Mead, A. R., "Functional Program at the Master's Degree Level for Teachers and School Administrators." *Educational Administration and Supervision.* 36:107-12, Feb., 1950.

Merritt, C. B., "Requirements for Master's Degrees in Education." *Journal of Educational Research.* 49:235-38, Nov., 1955.

Middlebrook, L. R., "Higher Learning and Literary Scholarship." *South Atlantic Quarterly.* 49:53-58, Jan., 1950.

Miller, T. R., "Fifth-Year Program in Elementary Education." *New York State Education.* 35:379-82, Feb., 1948.

Mississippi State College. *College looks at its graduate program: Study in self-evaluation.* State College, Miss., The College, 1953.

Moore, B. V., "Educational Facilities and Financial Assistance for Graduate Students in Psychology, 1959-1960." *American Psychologist.* 1958, 13:741-60.

Moore, W. J., "Graduate Instruction at the Teacher-Education Level." *Kentucky School Journal.* 30:10-13, Dec., 1951.

Morgan, J. W., "Graduate Work in Industrial Education." *Industrial Arts and Vocational Education.* 41:158-59, May, 1952.

Murray, R. K., "Effect of a University's Graduate Program on Its Undergraduate Education." *Journal of Higher Education.* 32:260-64, May, 1961.

Nabrit, S. M., "Desegregation and the Future of Graduate and Professional Education in Negro Institutions." *Journal of Negro Education.* 27, No. 3:414-18, Summer, 1958.

National Catholic Educational Association. Commission on Graduate Study. *Graduate programs and degrees offered by Catholic institutions of higher learning in the United States.* St. Louis, Mo., Saint Louis University Graduate School, 1958. 16p.

National Education Association. Educational Policies Commission. *Higher education in a decade of decision.* (Edited by Herman B Wells.) Washington, The Association, 1957. 152p.

National Society for the Study of Education. *Fiftieth yearbook; pt. 1, graduate study in education.* (Edited by Nelson B. Henry.) Chicago, University of Chicago Press, 1951. Bibliography.

Ness, Frederic W., ed., *A guide to graduate study: Programs leading to the Ph.D. degree.* Second edition, revised and enlarged. Washington, American Council on Education, 1960. 457p.

Neudling, Chester L. and Blessing, James H., *Graduate general humanities programs.* (U. S. Office of Education. Bulletin 1960, No. 12) Washington, U. S. Government Printing Office, 1960. vi, 126p. Bibliography.

Newcomer, Mabel, *A century of higher education for American women.* New York, Harper, 1959. 266p.

"New Degrees at Rockford College." *School and Society.* 65:439, June 14, 1947.

"New M.A. in Education at Reed College." *School and Society.* 67:366, May 15, 1948.

Nock, Francis J., "Foreign Languages as Graduate Study Requirements." *College and University.* 33, No. 2:154-62, Winter, 1958.

North, A. A., "Why Is the American Catholic Graduate School Failing To Develop Catholic Intellectualism?" *National Catholic Educational Association Bulletin.* 53:179-89, Aug., 1956.

Painter, Theophilus S., "The Selection and Recruitment of Graduate Students." *Graduate Journal.* 1:41-50, Spring, 1958.

Park, M. G., "New Trend Graduate Program for Elementary School Teachers." *Journal of Educational Research.* 42:667-77, May, 1949.

Paulsen, F. R., "Graduate Interdisciplinary Seminars for Educational Administrators." *Educational Research Bulletin.* 40:8-11, Jan., 1961.

Phelps, R. H., "Issues in Graduate Education." *Institute of International Education News Bulletin.* 32:22-24, Jan., 1957.

Pierson, M. B., *Graduate work in the South.* Chapel Hill, N. C., University of North Carolina Press, 1947. Bibliography.

Praxedes, Sister Mary, "Practice and Opinions on Master's Nonresearch Degrees." *School and Society.* 75:72-74, Feb. 2, 1952.

Preston, Malcolm H., "Hofstra College: M.A. in Humanities Program." In: Neudling, Chester L. and Blessing, James H., *Graduate general humanities programs.* Washington, U. S. Government Printing Office, 1960. pp. 75-82.

"Problems and Policies of Graduate Education: A Symposium." *Journal of Higher Education*. 30:119-45, March, 1959. Bibliography.

Pyle, W. H., "Graduate School." *Journal of Higher Education*. 17:141-45, March, 1946.

Quain, E. A., "Problems for Catholic Graduate Schools Created by New Population Trends." *National Catholic Educational Association Proceedings*. 1953:212-18.

Radcliffe College. Radcliffe Committee on Graduate Education for Women. *Graduate education for women: The Radcliffe Ph.D.* (Bernice B. Cronkhite, Chairman.) Cambridge, Mass., Harvard University Press, 1956. 135p.

Ragazzini, J. R., "Requirements of a Graduate Curriculum." *Journal of Engineering Education*. 39:241-43, Dec., 1948.

Raimy, V. C., ed., *Training in clinical psychology.* (The Boulder Conference Report.) New York, Prentice-Hall, 1950.

Redd, G. N., "Resources for Graduate Work for Negroes in the States of Alabama, Kentucky, and Tennessee." *Journal of Negro Education*. 15:161-71, April, 1946.

Reed, G. A., "Fifty Years of Conflict in the Graduate School." *Educational Record*. 33:5-23, Jan., 1952. Bibliography.

Reedy, S. J., "Graduate Work in Selected White and Negro Institutions." *Journal of Negro Education*. 14:256-58, April, 1945.

Regan, R., "Scholarships for Graduate Scholars." *National Catholic Educational Association Bulletin*. 56: 152-56, Aug., 1959.

Reynolds, G. F., "Oral Interpretation as Graduate Work in English." *College English*. 11:204-10, Jan., 1950.

Richardson, H. D., "Educational Research Requirements for the Master's Degree." In: American Educational Research Association. *Improving educational research; official report*, 1948. pp. 213-18.

Robinson, H. M., "New Graduate Programs." *Elementary School Journal*. 60: 422-27, May, 1960.

Rock, G. D., "Some Challenges Facing Catholic Graduate Education in the Next Half-Century." *National Catholic Educational Association Proceedings*. 1953: 205-8.

Rosenhaupt, Hans W. and Chinlund, Thomas J., *Graduate students: Experience at Columbia University, 1940-1956.* New York, Columbia University Press, 1958. xi, 125p.

Roth, J. A., "Faculty Conception of Success in Graduate Study." *Journal of Higher Education*. 26:350-56+, Oct., 1955.

Sarah Lawrence College. Committee on Graduate Studies. *Graduate program in an undergraduate college: The Sarah Lawrence experience.* (Edited by Charles Trinkaus.) Middletown, Conn., Wesleyan University Press, 1956. xx, 119p.

Schmidt, George P., *The liberal arts college: A chapter in American cultural history.* New Brunswick, N. J., Rutgers University Press, 1957. 310p.

Scott, H. A., "Graduate Instruction in Physical Education." *Teachers College Record*. 50:247-57, Jan., 1949. Bibliography.

Seashore, C. E., "Advanced Degrees in Music." *Music Educators Journal*. 31:34+, April, 1945.

———, "Advanced Degrees in Speech." *Journal of Higher Education*. 16:378-81, Oct., 1945.

————, "Terminal Programs in the Graduate Schools." *Science.* 102:213-15, Aug. 31, 1945.

See, H. W., "Psychological Testing as Part of the Master's-Degree Program in Education." *North Central Association Quarterly.* 30:299-301, Jan., 1956.

Shuck, E. C., *Practices in administering the master's thesis in 177 American graduate schools.* Bowling Green, Ohio, The Author, 1949.

Sibley, E., "Education of Social Science Teachers." *Journal of General Education.* 3:113-20, Jan., 1949.

Simon, C. T., "Graduate Study in Speech." *Quarterly Journal of Speech.* 36: 462-70, Dec., 1950. Bibliography.

Smith, W. E., "Terminal Master's Degrees." *Progressive Education.* 32:103-8, July, 1955.

Snell, John L. and others, *European history in the South.* New Orleans, La., Tulane University Graduate School, 1959. Bibliography.

Southern Association of Colleges and Secondary Schools. Commission on Institutions of Higher Education. "Report. Committee on Graduate Study." *Southern Association Quarterly.* 12:222-35, Feb., 1948.

Speer, D. G., "For Standardized Graduate Language Requirements." *Modern Language Journal.* 41:292-93, Oct., 1957.

Spivey, Herman E., "The Role of the Graduate School in the Promotion of Scholarship." *Graduate Journal.* 1:144-54, Fall, 1958.

Stabler, E., "Master of Arts in Teaching at Wesleyan University." *Journal of Teacher Education.* 6:143-48, June, 1955.

————, "Master of Arts in Teaching Idea." *Educational Record.* 41:224-29, July, 1960.

————, "Master of Arts in Teaching Program: A Survey of Graduates." *Journal of Teacher Education.* 8:81-83, March, 1957.

Staley, S. C., "Report on the Père Marquette Physical Education Graduate Study Conference." In: College Physical Education Association. *Fifty-second Annual Proceedings,* 1949. pp. 77-81.

Staudt, V. M., "Graduate Schools Ought To Train Teachers of Psychology." *Journal of Genetic Psychology.* 90:271-74, June, 1957.

Stewart, M. A., "Organization of the Graduate School." *Journal of Higher Education.* 30:136-40, March, 1959.

Stewart, Ward, *Graduate study in public administration.* A guide to graduate programs. (U. S. Office of Education. Circular No. 631.) Washington, U. S. Government Printing Office, 1961. xi, 158p.

Stoke, Harold W., "Future of Graduate Education." *Journal of Higher Education.* 18:473-77+, Dec., 1947.

————, "Some Observations on Graduate Study." *Journal of Higher Education.* 25:287-91+, June, 1954.

Storr, Richard J., *The beginnings of graduate education in America.* Chicago, University of Chicago Press, 1953. ix, 195p.

Strothmann, F. W. On behalf of the Committee of Fifteen. *The graduate school today and tomorrow.* New York, Fund for the Advancement of Education, 1955. 42p.

"Survey of Graduate Schools." *Higher Education.* 16:11-12, May, 1960.

Taylor, Hugh, *Graduate education at Princeton, 1945 to 1958.* Princeton, N. J., The University, 1959. 29p.

181

"Teacher Training as the Primary Aim of the Graduate Training Program." *School and Society.* 69:70, Jan. 29, 1949.

Thecla, Sister Mary, "Co-operative Graduate Programs: Actualities and Possibilities." *National Catholic Educational Association Bulletin.* 56:179-82, Aug., 1959.

"Thoughts on the Thesis: Master of Arts." *Times Educational Supplement.* 2228: 145, Jan. 31, 1958.

University of Southern California Graduate School. *Graduate studies in a world reborn.* Los Angeles, Calif., The University, 1945.

Van Valkenburg, S., "Graduate Training in Geography." *Journal of Geography.* 47:219-27, Sept., 1948.

Viens, Claude P. and Wadsworth, Philip, "Foreign Language Entrance and Degree Requirements for the M.A., M.S., and Ph.D. Degrees." *Publications of the Modern Language Association.* 72:22-32, Sept., 1957.

Wahlquist, J. T., "Graduate School." In: Valentine, P. F., ed., *American College.* New York, Philosophical Library, 1949. pp. 516-69. Bibliography.

Walters, E., "What Degree for College Teachers?" *Journal of Higher Education.* 31:69-74, Feb., 1960. Bibliography.

Warren, A. and Wellek, R., "Study of Literature in the Graduate School: Diagnosis and Prescription." *Sewanee Review.* 55:610-26, Oct., 1947.

Watson, C. M. and Richey, R. W., *Present practices and trends in the preparation of elementary school principals at the graduate level.* Bloomington, Ind., Indiana University Bookstore, 1955.

Weaver, J. C., "Facts and Philosophy of Graduate Extension Education." *Educational Record.* 40:242-48, July, 1959.

——, "Federal Aid to Research and Graduate Education." *Journal of Higher Education.* 30:146-54, March, 1959.

——, "Off-Campus Graduate Education." In: *Proceedings of the Midwest Conference on Graduate Study and Research.* 15th Annual Meeting, 1959. pp. 1-12.

——, *Some dilemmas in graduate education: A report to the Carnegie Corporation of New York on a travelling fellowship, 1957-1958.* New York, Carnegie Corporation of New York, 1958. 69p.

Wilt, N., "Higher Degrees and Lower Standards." *Journal of General Education.* 10:99-103, April, 1957.

Winters, C. L., Jr., "Off-campus Graduate Centers: A Problem of University Adult Education." *Adult Education.* 10, No. 2:94-100, Winter, 1960.

Winters, M. and McGill, E. C., "Study of Thesis Requirements for the Master's Degree in Business Education." In: National Association of Business Teacher-Training Institutions. *Bulletin.* No. 48, pp. 70-80.

Wirth, A. G., "Role of Courses in Education at the Level of the Master's Degree." *National Association of Secondary-School Principals Bulletin.* 40:104-7, May, 1956.

Wish, Harvey, "Degrees in American Culture." *Journal of Higher Education.* 19: 137-40+, March, 1948.

Yates, G. F., "Vital Subject Areas for Catholic Graduate School Endeavor." *National Catholic Educational Association Proceedings.* 1953:209-11.

Zetler, R. L. and Crouch, W. G., "Graduate School in General Education." *Journal of Higher Education.* 21:239-42, May, 1950.

182